Library of
Davidson College

THE SOVIET THREAT TO NATO'S NORTHERN FLANK

THE SOVIET THREAT
TO
NATO'S NORTHERN FLANK

Marian K. Leighton

*The Soviet Threat to
NATO's Northern Flank*

Agenda Paper No. 10

*Copyright © 1979 by National Strategy Information
Center, Inc.
111 East 58th Street
New York, N.Y. 10022*

No part of this publication may be reproduced,
stored in a retrieval system, or transmitted
in any form or by any means, electronic,
mechanical, photocopying, recording,
or otherwise, without the prior
written permission of the publisher.

ISBN: 0-87855-803-9

LC 79-89361

Printed in the United States of America

Table of Contents

Preface *vii*
  Frank R. Barnett

The Soviet Threat to NATO's Northern Flank 1
  Marian K. Leighton

NSIC Agenda Papers 97

NSIC Strategy Papers 98

Other NSIC Publications 100

Preface

In an opening round of World War II, after Stalin's cynical 1939 Pact with Hitler had failed to avert Nazi Germany's 1941 attack on the Soviet Union, the hard pressed Churchill welcomed Russia as an ally, saying, "the enemy of my enemy is my friend." If both in logic and history this proved to be a disorienting overstatement, at the time there were few doubters. The U.S. extended massive Lend-Lease assistance to the Soviet Union before and after December 1941. A great ocean supply train crossed the North Atlantic, braved crippling Nazi attacks, and landed untotaled hundreds of millions of dollars of war supplies at Russia's ice-free Arctic Circle port of Murmansk on the Kola Peninsula, the only available port at that time. The run to what has now become, as Dr. Leighton points out, "the world's largest city north of the Arctic Circle" convinced the Russians of the strategic importance of the port and its surrounding hinterland. Thus, they have proceeded in a variety of ways to apply the lessons of Murmansk, learned during the "Great Patriotic War," to the Soviet grand strategy for the current protracted conflict.

The Murmansk Oblast, extended by Petsamo, now Pechenga, the port territory Russia severed from defeated Finland, has become the largest Fleet (and Air Arm) base of the Soviet Union. It borders on Norway's North Cape and, in effect, overlooks the northern boundary areas of Finland and Sweden. It is from this great naval and air base that the Russians have conducted their successful entry through the so-called Greenland Gap (past the Norwegian Sea, the United Kingdom, and Iceland) into the Atlantic Ocean. Supplemented by the Baltic Fleet based at Kaliningrad and Leningrad, this Soviet Northern Fleet demonstrated in its highly successful world-wide *Okean* naval exercises of 1970 and 1975 that the Russians could easily deploy their superfleet capability into the Atlantic and anywhere else in the great Oceans of the planet. The Bear had learned to swim with global strength.

It is also worth noting that the whole Kola Peninsula—the Murmansk Oblast—has become an important mining and industrial area sustaining, repairing, and refurbishing its warfooting population and product. It is connected by a 900-mile rail line to Leningrad and, of perhaps even greater significance, to the White Sea-Baltic Canal* capable of transiting ballistic missile boats, submarines, and more conventional sea-borne traffic.

NATO's Northern Flank—Iceland, Norway, Denmark, the United Kingdom, and West Germany—faces with inadequate defensive means and declining political cohesion this formidable Soviet opponent buttressed by its Baltic Warsaw Pact allies, Poland and East Germany. The imbalance in military force, to the disadvantage of NATO's Northern Flank, could offer Moscow the opportunity to drive political wedges between disparate partners by military diplomacy or "armed coercion." Dr. Leighton warns of the "establishment of a special atmosphere in which Soviet wishes will be respected by reflex in the Nordic states," an atmosphere which, if unchecked, would permit Moscow "to dominate the region without resorting to war."

Soviet military "diplomacy" operates in a variety of yet uncountered ways:

1. East German and Polish naval and air bases in the Western Baltic have been increasingly utilized by the growing Soviet Baltic Fleet. Thus, the reality is that safe transit of

---

*Alexandr I. Solzhenitzen tells us in the second volume of *The Gulag Archipelago* that the canal was originally built in some twenty months from September 1931 to April 1933 by forced labor with little or no mechanized equipment and that perhaps as many as 250,000 "prisoners" died of deprivation and hardships during its construction. In the 1950s it was modernized after suffering from war damage. In the 1970s it was further enlarged, permitting the Northern and Baltic Fleets to reinforce each other without surveillance from NATO's installations on Norway's North Cape or from ships and aircraft operating from Norway's Svalbard (Spitsbergen) Archipelago in the Barents Sea.

the Danish Straits can no longer be guaranteed to NATO forces even if the neutral Swedish Navy were added to NATO's Baltic capacity. Denmark and a potentially outflanked NATO central front are at risk.
2. Norway continues to be a special target of Soviet and East German political assault. Norwegians are bluntly advised to disengage from NATO, to cease and desist from non-existent "military aggressive preparations," to shun the deployment of the neutron bomb, to join Sweden and especially Finland in campaigning for a Nordic "zone of peace and neutrality" free of nuclear weapons, etc.
3. Displaying their military "big stick," the Soviets practice constant harassment on border issues relating to (a) Norway's Svalbard Archipelago (Spitsbergen) and the dividing line on the Barents Sea between Norway and the USSR, (b) Sweden and the USSR over the island of Gotland, and (c) Denmark and Poland over the island of Bornholm.

In *The Soviet Threat to NATO's Northern Flank,* Dr. Leighton concludes with a quotation from Dr. Robert Weinland: "World War III may not be won on the northern flank, but it could definitely be lost there. If the USSR's expanding naval power, increasingly offensive-oriented airpower, and ground forces in the region convince the Nordic countries that U.S. power 4,000 miles distant is no match for Soviet strength in place, the war could be lost even before a shot is fired." In summary, it is clear that the Soviets seek to isolate and neutralize, if not control, NATO's Northern Flank.

Marian K. Leighton (B.A., Barnard; M.A. and Certificate of the Russian Institute and Ph.D., Columbia) has for the past twelve years concentrated on Russian and Soviet studies, writing, editing, and translating for Macmillan, the Columbia University Press, the U.S. Government (United States Information Office, Department of Commerce Joint Publications Research Service), and for Radio Liberty. Hers is a dependable scholarship based on thorough knowledge of original sources. The National Strategy Information Center is pleased to bring her obvious abilities to a wider audience.

A subsequent NSIC publication, written by an informed military analyst from Turkey, will offer a similar analysis of the threats to NATO's Southern Flank.

> Frank R. Barnett, *President*
> National Strategy Information Center, Inc.

November 1979

The Soviet Threat to NATO's Northern Flank

If our northern flank should be turned, America's access to Europe would be exposed and thus her ability to aid us would be curtailed. NATO's northern flank is an area whose importance is growing.... Its defense is vital to the very survival of the West as a whole.
General Sir Walter Walker, former Commander-in-Chief
of Allied Forces, Northern Europe
Quoted in the *New York Times,* December 15, 1971

In a recent article on the growing Soviet military threat, *U.S. News and World Report* cited six particularly dangerous areas where events could trigger a Soviet-American confrontation. One of them was Norway, where, the magazine pointed out, the USSR seeks control of the vital sea route between its huge military base at Murmansk and the open Atlantic.

The mention of Norway as such a volatile area must have caught much of the general reading public by surprise. While Western policymakers and media have been preoccupied with the military balance on the Central Front and with the ramifications of the Greco-Turkish dispute for the viability of NATO's southern flank, the northern theater, to which Norway is the key, has failed to receive the attention it deserves. This region[1] has become all the more significant with the recent upgrading of the Russian base complex on the Kola

---

[1] *The Military Balance, 1977–78* (London: International Institute for Strategic Studies, 1977), p. 102, notes that "the Northern European Command [AFNORTH] covers not only Norway but also the Baltic area—including Denmark, Schleswig-Holstein, and the Baltic Approaches—which is intimately linked with the Central sector." AFNORTH's headquarters are located at Kolsaas, near Oslo. Under AFNORTH is the Joint Baltic Command (COMBALTAP), which consists of Danish and West German forces.

Peninsula, just 200 miles off the tip of northeastern Norway. Available evidence suggests that the Russians intend to amass such overwhelming regional strength that the northern European countries' will to resist Soviet intimidation will be paralyzed. Should such intimidation fail—or in the event of a sudden deterioration of the international situation—the Soviet forces would be available to occupy adjacent areas as buffer zones for further offensive or defensive operations. In the meantime, the very presence of the Soviet forces has had tangible repercussions on the domestic political scene of the northern flank countries. Moscow's conviction that military strength yields important political dividends seems to be vindicated. As one analyst recently pointed out, "while on the Southern Flank there is rising Western concern about the military consequences of political instabilities, on the Northern Flank that Western concern must be directed toward the political and psychological consequences of growing military instabilities."[2]

This paper will examine the growing Soviet pressure against NATO's northern flank in general and Norway in particular and will focus on the urgency of tailoring Norwegian defense to the changing dimensions of the external threat and to the needs of NATO as a whole.

For the purpose of this study, it is useful to speak of two military theaters affecting Norway: the "northern theater," where Soviet naval forces based on the Kola Peninsula are capable of disrupting the reinforcement of Norway by its NATO allies, and the "southern theater," where Russia's Baltic Fleet and armies based at Kaliningrad can severely hamper the operations of West German troops assigned to aid Norway. These two theaters are, of course, not mutually exclusive; in fact, the Soviets may attempt simultaneously to neutralize air and naval bases and electronic surveillance systems in the far north and to block the Baltic approaches from the south. In this monograph, however, the theaters are separated arbitrar-

---

[2] Kenneth A. Myers, *North Atlantic Security: The Forgotten Flank?* (Washington, D.C.: Center for Strategic and International Studies, 1979), p. 62.

ily in order to better highlight the special problems each presents for military planners. In discussing the "northern theater," it will be necessary to mention, albeit briefly, the positions of Finland, Sweden, and Iceland; similarly, treatment of the "southern"—or "Baltic"—theater must include Denmark.

Norway as the Guardian of the Northern Flank

To appreciate Norway's key importance to NATO, one need only glance at recent history. Just as the occupation of Norway (and Denmark) by Nazi Germany was a vital prerequisite for the subsequent attack on the USSR—notably Leningrad—so now the "Finlandization" or control of Norway by the Kremlin would be a prelude to applying decisive pressure on Germany, NATO's heartland. World War II also indicated the supreme importance of coordination between the Soviet Union's northern and Baltic-based military forces. Weakness in this context nearly cost Russia the war and has now been corrected. The resulting emergence of the USSR's northwestern theater of operations (TVD)[3] as a strategic entity in its own right, with recently improved means of linking its Baltic, North and Norwegian Sea, and Atlantic Ocean components, constitutes an unprecedented danger for Norway and NATO's own northern flank.

The task of defending Norway entails two sets of considerations. One, which Stalin would have lumped under the term "permanently operating factors," is the country's peculiar geographic and geopolitical situation. Norway sits astride the vital North Atlantic routes linking Europe and the United States; it is one of Europe's smallest nations in terms of population but one of the largest territorially; the 25 percent of its

---

[3] See John Erickson, "The Northern Theater: Soviet Capabilities and Concepts," *Strategic Review,* Summer 1976, p. 2. In Soviet parlance, a TVD *(teatr voennykh deistvii)* is a subsection of a theater of war *(teatr voiny).* Thus, for example, the northwestern TVD is a component of the European theater. The forces in a TVD, or theater of military operations, are self-contained but are designed to perform missions within the overall context of Russia's European strategy.

area north of the Polar Circle is sparsely settled and particularly difficult to defend; Norway has an extremely long coastline; and, perhaps most importantly, the country shares a 150-mile-long border with the USSR.[4] Norway lies along the Soviet Northern Fleet's access route to the Atlantic and on the Warsaw Pact's maritime route to the Baltic via the North Sea. The Arctic Ocean between northern Norway and the Svalbard Archipelago is warmed by the Gulfstream and offers the Soviet fleet year-round access to European waters. As in World War II, however, hostile forces in northern Norway can harass Soviet naval operations out of Murmansk, while those in southern Norway can hinder Warsaw Pact movements through the Baltic exits. Moreover, during the winter months the southward extension of the polar ice forces Soviet naval vessels to operate within the Norwegian 200-mile zone.

The other central aspect of Norwegian defense concerns the changing international environment since Norway became a charter member of NATO in 1949. In particular, U.S. and British maritime supremacy has been seriously eroded by the emergence of the Soviet Union as a formidable naval power. The Northern Fleet, which in times past was Russia's smallest and weakest naval arm, is now its largest and most dangerous. The fleet's exercise area, moreover, has been extended from the Barents Sea westward into the Norwegian Sea and even the North Sea in recent years. Other new trends also weigh heavily on Norwegian defense officials. The Barents Sea has become an arena of friction in the wake of oil discoveries.

Questions over demarcation of the continental shelf and over fishing rights have exacerbated Soviet-Norwegian relations. The status of Svalbard (Spitsbergen), where the USSR seeks a joint condominium with Norway, is another focus of dispute. Given the overwhelming power differential between Norway and the Soviet Union, such an arrangement would be

---

[4] The common border results from a Soviet-Finnish treaty of February 10, 1947, by which Finland ceded territory lost in wartime as well as additional territory along what is now the Norwegian-Soviet frontier.

tantamount to Soviet control of Svalbard and the strategically vital northern waters surrounding it.

Although the quarrels over oil and other resources in the Arctic are not as important to the Soviet Union as is Norway's relationship to NATO, they provide Moscow with an opportunity to exert pressure on Oslo and to exploit the political forces within the country who favor neutrality or purely Scandinavian cooperation rather than NATO membership. These forces desire, above all, to avoid friction with their powerful next-door neighbor.

Norway's traditional methods of resolving differences with Russia quietly and of avoiding provocations have encountered increasing difficulty as Moscow adopts a more brazen attitude (exemplified by failure to brief Oslo on a Soviet helicopter crash on Spitsbergen and by Premier Aleksei Kosygin's sharp attack, during a recent meeting of Nordic prime ministers in Helsinki, on Norway's "provocative" foreign policy).

Kosygin's accusations notwithstanding, Norwegian policy has exhibited remarkable restraint vis-à-vis the USSR. Norway joined NATO only on condition that no foreign troops or military bases would be harbored on the country's territory in peacetime, that no allied air or naval activity east of 24°E. longitude would be permitted, and that no allied maneuvers would be staged in the northernmost county of Finnmark. The Norwegian government later forbade the deployment of nuclear weapons in the country. In addition, Oslo has given notice of major military exercises on Norwegian soil and has conducted them along relatively predictable lines, with an accent on defensive rather than offensive operations. More recently, in concurrence with the Final Act of the Helsinki Conference on Security and Cooperation in Europe, Norway has invited Warsaw Pact observers to these exercises. Oslo continues to announce forthcoming military maneuvers even if they do not reach the 25,000-man threshold dictated by the Helsinki accords. With regard to the strategically sensitive Barents Sea, Norway has restricted offshore oil drilling operations north of latitude 62°N. to its own state-controlled oil companies.

In an interview with the conservative daily *Aftenposten* on January 2, 1978, Norwegian Foreign Minister Knut Frydenlund declared that "we belong to NATO, but during the formulation of our defense policy we have taken as much account of the Soviet Union as can be reasonably expected of a country's government. Our base policy, nuclear policy and severe restrictions on military maneuvers all constitute what, in Helsinki terminology, we call confidence-inspiring measures. And they're unilateral Norwegian measures."

If modifications in these policies of restraint are contemplated, they will result not, as Moscow contends, from "imperialist" warmongering or "outside [i.e., NATO] pressure" on Oslo, but from alarming Soviet military activity in Norway's immediate vicinity. One aspect of this activity centers upon the expanding Soviet base complex on the Kola Peninsula. Although the Kola forces must be viewed in the context of Soviet global strategy rather than primarily as a juggernaut against Norway, there are "tactical forces deployed to protect the bases and embodying the capability of seizing and holding any appreciable territorial buffer zone in order to guarantee that selfsame 'protection.' "[5] Moreover, the Soviet Union has greatly bolstered its amphibious landing capability, which serves *prima facie* as a regional instrument of power and thus poses a direct threat to Norway. Another dimension of Soviet military activity around Norway involves the appearance of new weapons systems and ominous maneuvers in both the "northern" and "Baltic" theaters, accompanied frequently by verbal threats and diplomatic pressures.

The Kola Peninsula and Russia's Northern Fleet

Even when one allows for Russia's alleged paranoia where defense is concerned, the buildup on the Kola Peninsula far exceeds the requirements for a strictly defensive role ("unless one accepts 'defense in depth' in terms of a secured and en-

---

[5] Erickson, "The Northern Theater," p. 2.

larged geographic zone and the domination of contiguous waters").[6] The naval and air components of the buildup in particular reflect the Soviet posture of forward deployment, which, in relation to the northern flank, may already have placed Norway behind the Soviet front lines. Also of great significance are the accelerating emplacement of infrastructure that is applicable for both military and economic purposes and the drive to promote colonization, industrialization, transportation, and communications links and the overall economic modernization of the Kola region. This activity, in turn, should be viewed in combination with the ambitious new "virgin lands" program, an attempt to raise agricultural yields by 50 percent as well as to consolidate small towns into larger cities and to speed industrialization in the vast "non-black-earth zone" stretching from the Arctic frontier southward beyond Moscow and from the Baltic states westward to the Urals. The total picture is one of building a secure rear base for defense in depth as well as for possible thrusts beyond the northern and Baltic boundaries.

Since the beginning of World War II, the population of the Murmansk Oblast and the Kola Peninsula has more than tripled—from about 300,000 to 1 million—and growth continues. The city of Murmansk has doubled in population—to 300,000 —since 1939. A vital unloading and transshipment point for seaborne Allied reinforcements to the Russian front in World War II, Murmansk—the world's largest city north of the Arctic Circle—retains its strategic significance as a virtually ice-free port and a point of egress for Soviet naval forces.[7] In addition, Murmansk is the terminus of the 900-mile railroad from Leningrad and of the Northeast Passage across the Arctic and is an important economic center, providing 20 percent of the USSR's fish products, as well as metals, timber, and raw materials for the fertilizer industry. Shipbuilding and repair

---

[6] *Ibid.*, p. 6.
[7] In 1977 the USSR published a book on the role of Murmansk in the defense of the Soviet Far North during the "Great Patriotic War"—with lessons implied for today. See S. I. Kabanov, *Pole boya—bereg* (Moscow: Voenizdat, 1977).

yards, sawmills, fish canneries, breweries, and textile and metal alloy factories are among the city's industries. The oblast has apatite, nickel, and some uranium mines, and ore processing is a major economic activity.

Urbanization is proceeding apace in the Murmansk region, notably in the dozen or more towns clustered along the Murmansk-Leningrad railway (there is also a direct rail link with Moscow). Not only the Kola Peninsula itself but also the adjacent areas are reaping the fruits of sustained Soviet investment. One example is Arkhangelsk. An important fishing and shipbuilding center, the city, with about 350,000 people, also has industries that produce paper and pulp, turpentine, resin, cellulose, building materials, and prefabricated houses. It should be noted in passing that the numerous Soviet fishing trawlers, merchant vessels, and other civilian ships operating out of Murmansk and Arkhangelsk could be used as troop carriers to help launch a surprise attack on the northern flank.

Murmansk Oblast was enlarged at the end of World War II with the incorporation of the city of Pechenga (the former Finnish Petsamo), which has both strategic and economic significance. A wartime supply base in the German-Finnish drive against Murmansk, the city is an ice-free port at the head of the Pechenga Fjord on the Barents Sea. It serves as a principal home port for Northern Fleet warships, a base for a Soviet naval infantry brigade, and an exercise area for Soviet amphibious units. It is the northern terminus of an Arctic highway, the base for a large herring fleet, and the site of valuable nickel, copper, and uranium mines. The Soviets have enlisted Finland's assistance in developing the northwestern corner of the USSR, including the area along the Soviet-Finnish border.

Much of the shipbuilding and repairing activity in and around the Kola Peninsula is, of course, military-related. It has been said that the submarine yards at Severodvinsk alone have an annual output equal to that of all U.S. submarine-building facilities combined. Ballistic missiles for the submarines are produced at Severomorsk, which also serves as headquarters for the commander-in-chief of the Northern Fleet and as a base for surface combatants. The fleet's chief base is at Polyarnoje, a satellite port of Murmansk, on the western coast of the Kola Fjord. Nearby is Rosta, a major repair facility for warships.

The military buildup on the Kola Peninsula apparently results from the discovery during the "Great Patriotic War" of serious vulnerabilities in that sector, as well as from the realization that the region's ice-free ports afford the only exit point for the strategic naval forces designed to fight a war against NATO Europe and the United States. Since the top-priority goal of Moscow's foreign policy is the destruction of NATO and the separation of the United States from Western Europe —which would then be ripe for neutralization or incorporation into the Soviet orbit—the forces assigned to achieve that goal have received preferential attention. As new ships (especially submarines) and aircraft enter the Soviet inventory, they are usually attached first to the Kola bases. About 170 submarines, of which more than half are nuclear-powered, are homeported with the Northern Fleet. This figure represents nearly 75 percent of the USSR's nuclear-powered ballistic-missile-carrying submarines (SSBNs). In addition, the Northern Fleet has approximately 5000 surface vessels, including 60 major surface combatants.

According to an article in the West German magazine *Der Spiegel* of August 4, 1978, the USSR's first aircraft carrier, the *Kiev,* "is the flagship of the Arctic Sea Fleet, equipped with up to 20 antisubmarine helicopters of the 'Hormone' type and with 12 vertical takeoff planes of the YAK-36 type." The article adds that the *Minsk,* the second such carrier, will also be assigned to the Northern Fleet and that by 1985 a third carrier (out of an expected total of six) will also join that fleet. Similarly, there is a strong possibility that the Soviet Union's first nuclear-powered surface warship and future sister ships will go to the Northern Fleet. The first Rogov-class amphibious landing ship—the largest of its kind in the Soviet Navy—was assigned to the Northern Fleet. Many of the surface components of the fleet are undergoing modernization—e.g., the replacement of gun with missile units—but the fleet's actual expansion in recent years has occurred overwhelmingly in the area of strategic missile submarines.

- The Northern Fleet is responsible for the defense of the USSR's Arctic shore, including the vital military installations on the Kola Peninsula; for seizing and maintaining control of the Norwegian and Barents seas in order to protect the SSBNs deployed there and to screen the transit of Soviet submarines into the Atlantic; for prevention of logistical support and/or troop landings by NATO in Norway; for naval support in the form of extending the Soviet army's land flank seaward; and for coastal amphibious operations against Norway, Svalbard, and even Iceland. The amphibious role would be performed by the 1,900-man regiment of naval infantry assigned to the fleet and by army troops that periodically undergo amphibious training.[8] Units of the Northern Fleet might also participate in a battle for the approaches to the Baltic. Naval exercises and transfers of ships between the Northern and Baltic fleets result in a virtually continuous Soviet naval presence off Norway's coast.
- Soviet air power based on the Kola Peninsula has been strengthened in recent years and has assumed a complexion increasingly suited for offensive rather than defensive operations. There are close to 300 fighters and long-range bombers based at 40 airfields, as well as some 60 helicopters, 20 medium-range transport planes, and 55 maritime reconnaissance aircraft. Several hundred naval aircraft operate with the Northern Fleet, including about 150 Tu-16s and 30 Tu-22s, which are fitted for antiship and antisubmarine warfare roles. Although the Backfire bomber has been conspicuously absent from patrols over northern seas and thus may be experiencing problems, it will presumably be deployed on Kola in the near future. The MiG-23 Flogger fighter is already there. On the Kola Peninsula, as elsewhere, Soviet tactical airpower exhibits a "steady and relentless shift from air defense to strike mis-

---

[8] Information on the Northern Fleet has been gathered largely from Siegfried Breyer and Norman Polmar, *Guide to the Soviet Navy* (Annapolis, Md.: U.S. Naval Institute Press, 1977) and from *The Military Balance*.

sions." Deployment of the Su-19 Fencer is a prominent example.[9] Units of the Soviet Naval Air Force operate continuously over the Barents and Norwegian seas and the North Atlantic.

The ground force buildup on Kola has been less spectacular than that of the naval and air strike forces; but that is cold comfort for Norway, which has a mere 500 border guards at Kirkenes facing two Soviet motorized rifle divisions (totaling some 27,000 men) deployed between the Norwegian frontier and the Murmansk railway. These units are reportedly equipped with an abnormally large complement of vehicles fitted for rapid mobility across snow and are maintained in an extremely high state of readiness.[10] They are supported by surface-to-surface missiles known in the West as Scud, by SAM-4 antiaircraft missiles, and by an army artillery regiment. According to the most recent report seen by the author, there are five Soviet divisions deployed on the Kola Peninsula, in addition to two mobile army divisions (an apparent reference to the motorized rifle divisions) along the border. The total number of troops in place would thus be about 70,000.[11] Other contingents that can be brought to bear on Kola include at least three airborne divisions, a naval infantry brigade (based at Pechenga) of 3,000–4,000 men, and so-called naval pioneers, consisting largely of demolition experts and frogmen. Moreover, the ground and air forces in the area can be speedily and covertly reinforced. According to Norwegian officials, the Soviet ground troop strength along the frontier, backed by the 31st Tactical Air Army, constitutes the largest concentration of military force in the world.[12]

John Erickson has observed that the Kola Peninsula

> ... is essentially small and "cramped" against the Norwegian frontier. Shortage of real estate, however, does not

---

[9] See the *New York Times,* March 6, 1976.
[10] According to Erickson, "The Northern Theater," p. 4, these troops are "in Category I as first-line Soviet divisions maintaining full equipment and 85 percent or more of their war establishment."
[11] *New York Times,* April 23, 1978.
[12] *Ibid.,* June 20, 1977.

seem in itself any serious ground for a Soviet thrust into Norway to augment existing facilities, at least in terms of basing for submarines—though forward airfields might be another matter.... On the other hand, if the acquisition of bases does not provide a prime impulse for territorial incursion, the same compression and potential vulnerability demands assurance for the Soviet Union that contiguous Norwegian space areas are not used in any manner inimical to Soviet security interests—particularly radar or other surveillance systems, as well as missile (or antimissile) capabilities.[13]

Returning to the Northern Fleet, a new factor confronts Norwegian security calculations. Recent Soviet military expenditures have focused heavily on the strategic submarine force, the lion's share of which has been assigned to the Northern Fleet. Even more important, the increased range of the Soviet submarine-launched ballistic missiles (SLBMs) means that the Barents, Norwegian, and Greenland seas have all gained new significance as areas of patrol and passage for the submarines. The Delta-class boats are armed with SSN-8 missiles, which have a 4,200-nautical-mile range that permits them to strike targets in the United States without leaving "home" waters in the Barents. The Yankee-class submarines, armed with SSN-6 missiles, have only a 1,500-nautical-mile range and thus must move into the western half of the Atlantic to take up their firing stations. Like the Deltas, however, they use the Barents Sea as their chief area of peacetime deployment, exercise, and patrol. There are about 60 Deltas and 25 Yankees with the Northern Fleet.

Whether Russia's SSBNs will "flood' the Atlantic as the prelude to a general war or will be held in abeyance until a later stage of hostilities, their increasing numbers and capability magnify Norway's importance as a monitoring station. Norway's North Cape, situated on an island off Finnmark, may be one of the most strategic pieces of real estate in the

---

[13] Erickson, "The Northern Theater," p. 3.

world. Moreover, the whole area from Finnmark to the Svalbard Archipelago constitutes a major chokepoint for Soviet naval forces leaving Murmansk for the open ocean and is thus an exceedingly sensitive zone for Norway. This 400-mile stretch of the Barents Sea harbors a whole series of explosive crosscurrents: large-scale oil deposits; Soviet-Norwegian disputes over fishing rights and the limits of the continental shelf; frictions regarding Soviet activity on Spitsbergen; and, it seems, the makings of a "sanctuary" for Russian SSBNs. Norway's proverbial status as the "quiet corner of Europe" has ended with a vengeance.

Growing Soviet Probes in Norway's Northern Theater

Underlying tensions in Norway's Arctic theater have been brought to the surface by increasingly provocative Soviet behavior along the coasts. Soviet submarine probes of the Norwegian fjords date back a number of years but have intensified recently. Their apparent mission is to spy on submarine-detection devices installed there. In view of their so-called "9th of April complex," created by the surprise German landings from the sea on that date in 1940, the Norwegians are peculiarly wary of this Soviet naval activity. There have also been firings of unarmed Soviet ballistic missiles in the disputed waters of the Barents Sea. These firings, a blatant form of intimidation, occurred after Norway had conducted seismic probes for oil in the disputed area. *Aftenposten* called the Soviet action "a curious kind of negotiating tactic" and added that "good neighbors should have no need to demonstrate their military power to enter into a dialogue on such a complex problem."[14]

Soviet surface vessels, like submarines, have extended their maneuver area westward from the Barents into the Norwegian Sea. They have also been involved in many disturbing incidents. Moreover, during the summer of 1978 a number of

---
[14] Quoted in the *New York Times,* October 2, 1975.

Russian merchant ships stopped illegally inside Norway's four-mile territorial waters, citing excuses such as engine trouble, injury to crew members, or dangerous weather conditions, which turned out to be phony.[15] The incidents occurred chiefly in the Barents Sea off the Nordkyn and Varanger peninsulae in northeast Norway. Gamvik, on the Nordkyn Peninsula, is the terminus of a cable that links seabed sonar installations between Norway and Svalbard and is specifically used to monitor Soviet submarine activity. Thus, the ships were either studying the cable or, perhaps, dropping sonar devices of their own.[16] At any rate, the insolent attitude of the ship captains and the fact that the vessels tarried during the season of the midnight sun, when detection was unavoidable, prompted a high Norwegian official to comment, "We have reluctantly come to the conclusion that we are confronted with a pattern of deliberate activity. My own belief is that the Russians are engaged in a general probing of Norwegian attitudes and response capabilities." Defense Minister Rolf Hansen more bluntly termed the Soviet actions an example of "gunboat diplomacy."[17]

Svalbard has been another focus of suspicious Soviet military activity. A treaty signed in Paris in 1920 by Norway and some 40 other nations awarded sovereignty over the islands to Oslo but guaranteed all the signatories equal access to Svalbard's resources, guided by Norwegian law and regulations. In addition, the treaty forbade bases or permanent naval installations on Svalbard and declared that the archipelago "may never be used for warlike purposes." The USSR (which did not adhere to the treaty until the mid-1930s) is the only country besides Norway that has taken advantage of the access

---

[15] International law permits ships to sail through these waters but not to stop.
[16] One vessel, the Soviet cargo ship *Grumant*, was seen by a NATO reconnaissance plane hauling wires or lines out of the water while anchored inside the Norwegian territorial sea off Nordkyn. The plane arrived too late to see whether the lines had been thrown overboard by the crew or were being hauled in from the sea.
[17] *New York Times,* August 4, 1978.

clause.[18] Moreover, as early as 1944 Moscow unsuccessfully petitioned Oslo for joint Soviet-Norwegian administration and defense of the archipelago.

The Soviet Union's Arktikugol Company maintains coal-mining centers at Barentsburg and Pyramiden on Spitsbergen. Some 2,000 Russians live there, compared with only 1,000 Norwegians in Norway's coal-mining community some 35 miles away at Longyearbyen. (Both operations yield 450,000 tons of coal monthly.) Leif Eldring, a former governor of Spitsbergen and head of the new Polar Division of the Norwegian Ministry of Justice, contends that the Russians "don't really need the coal. They use it as an excuse to keep a presence [on Spitsbergen], to keep an eye on other people."[19] The same reasoning presumably explains why six Russians stay permanently at Svalbard's airport, which handles only one Aeroflot flight per month.

The Soviet and Norwegian mining communities coexisted peacefully until recent major changes in the strategic and economic environment of the Svalbard region sparked friction. These changes were caused by deployment of Soviet missile and hunter-killer submarines in the Barents Sea, by evidence of valuable undersea oil deposits, and by a mounting scarcity of fish, which is a staple in Nordic diets. Moscow's desire to protect its submarines from foreign scrutiny, to insure that foreign oil drilling operations do not obstruct the vital sea lanes, and to obtain what it considers a fair share of fishing rights in the region have led to proposals for joint Soviet-Norwegian rule over Svalbard—proposals tantamount to Soviet hegemony.

The USSR has resorted to such harassment tactics as refusal to use Norwegian postage in the islands or to supply a

---

[18] In August, 1977, Poland reportedly announced establishment of a "base for large expeditions conducting complex research in Spitsbergen." See *Survival*, January/February 1978, p. 43. In addition, Norwegian Foreign Minister Knut Frydenlund announced during an interview with *Aftenposten* on January 2, 1978 that a U.S. research team plans to duplicate the Arctic voyage of Norwegian explorer Fridtjof Nansen in the *Fram*—a project requiring U.S. construction of a supply station on Svalbard.
[19] *New York Times*, August 6, 1978.

list of Barentsburg and Pyramiden residents for income tax purposes, insisting instead on paying taxes in a lump sum. Thus, the Russian communities have become virtually autonomous enclaves, in violation of the 1920 Svalbard treaty. The Russians have also refused to recognize a special fishing zone established by Norway off Svalbard or to comply with Norwegian environmental regulations.[20] Safety standards for exploratory oil drilling have been flouted. In addition, the USSR failed to register a new power station at Barentsburg and embarked, without consulting the Norwegians, on a plan to build a fish-freezing plant there and to station nearby two trawlers (which regularly double as intelligence-gathering vessels).

Although the Norwegians reluctantly permitted six Soviet airline employees to stay permanently at Svalbard's new airport, Moscow antagonized Norway by failing to pay required airport taxes and fees on time and by staging the "wives episode," in which the spouses of four airport personnel were flown to Svalbard after Norway specifically vetoed family living accommodations near the airport. All these vexations, however, pale before mounting evidence of Soviet military activity on Svalbard.

First, Soviet military delegations disguised as mineral prospecting teams visited the islands, and the USSR began moving ships and aircraft in and out of Svalbard without Norwegian consent. Then, in 1975, an actual Soviet military colony was established at Kapp Heer, near Barentsburg, complete with electrified fencing, a road network, and round-the-clock security guards. Norwegians were forbidden to enter the area. A landing strip for helicopters was added more recently. Several helicopter crashes occurred on Svalbard, but the Russians failed to report them to Norwegian civil aviation authorities and hastily removed all instruments and other wreckage. On the night of August 21, 1978, helicopters secretly delivered the components of a mobile radar base that was established at

---

[20] A bizarre example of the latter occurred in April 1978, when a Soviet helicopter landed in the Southern Spitsbergen National Park (in violation of conservation statutes), removed a jeep from an abandoned Polish research station there, and transported it back to Barentsburg.

Kapp Heer. Had the equipment arrived on cargo ships, the Norwegians would have invoked the treaty and turned them back; but by the time the radar installation was discovered by a Norwegian reconnaissance plane it had become a *fait accompli.*

Close on the heels of the radar incident came the crash of a Soviet Tu-126 spy plane (the equivalent of the U.S. Airborne Warning and Control System, or AWACS, plane with "lookdown" radar) on the island of Hopen, off the Svalbard coast. A virtual Soviet task force of submarines, surface warships, reconnaissance and transport planes, fighter escorts, and helicopters carrying rescue teams converged on the area to hunt for the wreckage. Norwegians manning the lighthouse on Hopen sighted the debris first, however, and sent an encoded message to NATO's search headquarters. Soviet commando units were prevented from landing on Hopen's beach when a Norwegian naval patrol boat pulled the covers off its guns—a signal that it would fire on a landing party. Moscow was further embarrassed by Norway's refusal to return the plane's flight recorder and certain other bits of wreckage, pending investigation as to whether the Tu-126 had deliberately violated Norwegian airspace.

Moscow's response was to cancel a visit, scheduled for October 1978, of the Norwegian undersecretary of defense—a visit that would have included discussions about Soviet activities on Svalbard. The Russians also threatened to sever diplomatic relations with Norway.[21]

Studies of the flight recorder could reveal whether the aircraft had been maneuvering at various altitudes to test the range of the new Soviet radar at Kapp Heer. Many Norwegian officials believe that—far from serving as a mere navigational aid for helicopters—the radar might enable the USSR to control all air traffic on and around Svalbard.

On September 4, during the course of investigating the

---

[21] Norway's "victory" in the race to collect the AWACS wreckage was a coup comparable to that of Japan in gaining access to a MiG-25 Foxbat after its pilot defected. The flight recorder was eventually returned, and Undersecretary Holst visited Moscow in February 1979.

plane crash, Norwegian officials inspected the Soviet installations at Kapp Heer. They found construction underway to improve the helicopter platform, allegedly to facilitate landing under difficult weather conditions and with heavy loads. What aroused greater concern, however, was the type of MIL-8 helicopters used at the base. As a dispatch in *Aftenposten* noted on September 5:

> The MIL-8 is the Soviet Union's most widely used type of helicopter and is ... found in both military and civil versions. The helicopters at Kapp Heer have civil registration markings and are painted in Aeroflot colors, yet there is much to indicate that it is the MIL-8 version which is normally used as a troop transport and an attack helicopter. Open Western expert sources most frequently state that the civil MIL-8 has square windows, whereas the military version has round windows. Far more important, however, is a set of bolts and slots mounted on each side of the helicopter fuselage above the external fuel tanks. These bolts and slots correspond exactly with the points for mounting a ... stand which the military MIL-8 often has and which serves as a firing platform for several types of weapons, including the Soviet Union's standard 57-mm missiles. ... There is every indication that the civil MIL-8 very rarely has these installations. In any case, the conclusion must be that such firing platforms could be mounted on the helicopters at Kapp Heer without prior preparation.

Norwegian newspapers also featured reports, accompanied by photographs taken from the air, of Soviet construction of a landing strip on Svalbard for planes other than helicopters.

Many Norwegian officials fear that Moscow's next step will involve pressure for the demilitarization of the North Cape area, which is held by only a small Norwegian force and is virtually indefensible. Diplomatic pressure has already been exerted on Norway via Finland, which has proposed demilitarization of the entire Soviet-Norwegian frontier.

The combination of these varied Soviet military-political

pressures in the northern theater has badly shaken Norway's confidence in U.S. and NATO willingness to risk nuclear war on its behalf. Officials in the Carter Administration and the Pentagon, apparently awed by "the literal explosion of Soviet naval mobility" (to borrow the words of former NATO supreme commander Alexander Haig),[22] have already proposed a restriction of the U.S. Navy's wartime mission to exclude carrier-based air sorties and even troop landings on the Soviet mainland and to involve merely keeping open the sea lines of communication (SLOCs) between America and Europe. Navy Secretary W. Graham Claytor charged in a memorandum to Secretary of Defense Harold Brown that "a 'sea lanes' navy will not penalize the Soviets, will not hedge against the loss of Norway or the political loss of Iceland, and concedes the Norwegian Sea to the Soviets."[23] Insofar as the Navy shuns offensive operations, it will enable the Soviet fleet units in the Norwegian Sea to "create and sustain impressions of Soviet power and reduce the perceived efficacy of U.S. guarantees to Northern Europe."[24]

New Developments in the Baltic Theater

Increased Soviet military activity in the northern theater has its counterpart in the Baltic arena, where the USSR, assisted by its East German and Polish allies, has all but transformed this maritime gateway to Russia into a Communist lake. Warsaw Pact naval forces there outnumber NATO ships by four or five to one.

The Baltic Fleet in times past was the USSR's chief naval arm, but it suffers even more than its Northern counterpart from geographical constraints. While the Northern Fleet must break out of the Murmansk area through a series of "gaps" to reach the open ocean, the Baltic Fleet is subject to a bottling

---

[22] *U.S. News & World Report,* March 1, 1976, p. 38.
[23] *New York Times,* March 14, 1978.
[24] Johan Jørgen Holst, ed., *Five Roads to Nordic Security* (Oslo: Universitetsforlaget, 1973), p. 93.

up by Western naval forces that could mine or otherwise block the Baltic exits in the event of an East-West crisis. This situation goes far toward explaining why many of the Baltic Fleet's ships, especially submarines and ocean-going surface vessels, have been transferred in recent years to the Northern Fleet. Preventing the entry of NATO naval forces into the Baltic and keeping open the Baltic entrances for Warsaw Pact reinforcements are important missions of the Northern Fleet in the Baltic theater.

Major components of the Baltic Fleet include some 30 submarines (predominantly diesel-powered) and more than 60 major surface ships. Perhaps of greatest significance is the growing quantity and quality of Soviet amphibious and assault landing ships with the fleet. The improved ships of the Ropucha-class underwent trial voyages in the Baltic only a little more than two years ago; these vessels can carry 800 tons of cargo. The Alligator-class landing ships that operate with the fleet have a 1,700-ton carrying capacity. Now the Rogov-class ships, the largest ever built for the Soviet Navy, have appeared with the Baltic Fleet. With a cargo capacity of 5,100 tons, the Rogovs can accommodate both helicopters and hovercraft (landing craft operating on air cushions). According to a Western observer, "No Western navy at present has a similar capability. The ships, which are reportedly being built at the rate of three or four a year, can charge onto a beach at a speed of more than 45 mph and can land a platoon of soldiers with full equipment."[25]

A large, high-speed Soviet hovercraft capable of landing either up to 400 naval infantry troops or a mixture of infantry and tanks behind enemy lines has undergone testing near East Germany's island of Rügen in the Baltic. Another significant new addition to Soviet amphibious strength in the Baltic is a fast-moving roll-on/roll-off combination vehicle-and-container ship, which can transport and land sizable military

---

[25] See the *Christian Science Monitor,* November 13, 1978. The Ivan Rogov is smaller than the U.S.-built landing platform helicopter (LPH) but may be more versatile.

cargoes on large ramps without need of modern port facilities. The Soviet Navy has more than 20 Ro-Ro ferries, and more are reportedly on order; an undisclosed number operate with the Baltic Fleet. Also on order are two large, U.S.-designed SEABEE barge transport vessels, which can serve either in logistical and supply operations or as mother ships for landing craft. According to one report, the SEABEE, which Finnish shipyards are building, can land up to 25,000 tons of cargo—including 1,000-ton barges—in only 13 hours.[26] Soviet amphibious forces have already practiced unloading up to 700 T-72 tanks.[27]

The Baltic Fleet is designed mainly for local operations. Its major combat missions appear to be denial of the Baltic to NATO naval forces; seizure of the Danish Straits; logistical and amphibious operations in close support of the army, airborne troops, and other naval units; and attainment of control of the Baltic exits in order to maintain the waterway as a line of communications with Communist troops on the Central Front, to outflank NATO's forward defense in Central Europe, and to protect the flanks of the Warsaw Pact's ground troops there. A regiment of naval infantry and a sizable number of naval aircraft are attached to the Baltic Fleet. Nuclear-powered and missile-carrying submarines frequently join the fleet during training exercises.

The fleet's strength far exceeds what local requirements would warrant, even if the Swedish Navy were added to NATO forces in the Baltic. Evidence from Soviet naval exercises indicates, however, that the Baltic Fleet's operational commitments may now extend to the North Sea and parts of the Atlantic. The North Sea links the two vital areas of naval operations on the northern flank and serves as the conduit for bringing British reinforcements to the Continent. North Sea ports are also major terminals for U.S. troops and supplies destined for the northern flank.

Increasing Soviet and Warsaw Pact activity in the Baltic

---
[26] *Ibid.*
[27] *Manchester Guardian Weekly,* March 6, 1977.

presses particularly hard on Denmark (which, like Norway, has a "9th of April complex"). Of military as well as psychological significance is the fact that Denmark's island of Bornholm, which was occupied by Soviet troops from 1945 to 1947, is *east* of the East German border. A joint Soviet, East German, and Polish amphibious force permanently stationed in the Baltic could attack Denmark with an extremely high probability of success. "This is not to say that the Warsaw Pact powers necessarily intend to do so," states a British observer, "but it is a capability which they have chosen to acquire and which they did not possess before."[28] Moreover, the main fleet exercise areas for the Warsaw Pact navies that formerly were concentrated off the USSR's Baltic republics or near the Polish frontier have now edged westward to Rügen, which lies only 55 miles off Denmark. Still other exercises have taken place in the Kattegat near Zealand, the island on which Copenhagen stands. Circumnavigation of Denmark's islands has become virtually routine during Warsaw Pact training maneuvers. Although such ship movements could be interpreted as falling within the right of innocent passage, the vessels are not in transit but rather return eventually to their bases. A Danish military analyst points out that "activities that previously warned of hostile action have today become part of the normal scene, making the distinction between a naval exercise and an isolated attack against Denmark difficult. This in turn has reduced the early warning and reaction period."[29] Soviet surveillance from both sea and air of the Kattegat and Skagerrak has intensified, and Soviet naval patrol vessels and intelligence-gathering ships hover increasingly off the Danish coasts.

The trends of Communist naval activity in the northern and Baltic theaters display remarkable similarities. Just as units of the Northern Fleet have increasingly shifted their maneuvers from the Barents Sea westward into the Norwegian Sea and

---
[28] *Ibid.*, March 27, 1977.
[29] Orla Moller, "Danish Security Policy," *Atlantic Community Quarterly*, Fall 1977, p. 329.

thus closer to NATO Norway, so the Baltic Fleet components have shifted their maneuvers (notably amphibious landing exercises) westward toward NATO Denmark and the Baltic exits. And just as Soviet forces based on the Kola Peninsula are acquiring the capability for a smash-and-grab attack on northern Norway in wartime, so the Communist strength in the Baltic is becoming sufficient for a wartime breakthrough at the Oresund and the Great Belt leading from the Baltic to the North Sea. The overall trend in both theaters is toward reduced warning time for NATO and thus a lessened possibility for adequate reinforcement in case of emergency. (There is, incidentally, another parallel between Finnish proposals for a nuclear-free zone in northern Europe and Polish advocacy of turning the Baltic into a "sea of peace" and a "closed sea," thus excluding a military presence by the United States or other non-littoral states.)

According to a top official of the Danish military intelligence service, the East German and Polish fleets, like that of the USSR, have been strengthened, while the trend in the Danish fleet has been in the opposite direction.[30] East Germany and Poland have been particularly useful to Moscow in providing bases in the western Baltic that are far more favorable than the frequently icebound ports in the eastern sea and in opening their extensive shipbuilding, maintenance, and repair facilities to the USSR's Baltic Fleet.

Recent enlargement of the Baltic-White Sea canal has dramatically improved Soviet ability to coordinate the activities of the Northern and Baltic fleets, as well as to permit transit between the Kola bases and the naval maintenance and repair facilities in the Leningrad area without sailing either around Norway, where NATO monitoring devices record all Soviet naval movements, or through the Kattegat and the Øresund, where the Danish coast guard maintains constant surveillance. The canal, part of a complex network of Soviet internal waterways, is now large enough to accommodate destroyers and Hotel, Whiskey, and Golf-class submarines. NATO first wit-

---

[30] See the *New York Times,* February 16, 1975.

nessed Soviet efforts to coordinate naval operations in the northern and Baltic theaters during the *Sever* exercise in 1968; follow-ups occurred in the spring maneuvers of 1969 and especially during the worldwide *Okean* exercises of 1970 and 1975. Several other Soviet naval maneuvers have also emphasized theater coordination. During *Okean* 1975 an unprecedented number of Soviet naval units from the Baltic were deployed into the Atlantic. It should be noted that combined Northern-Baltic fleet operations also include air activity.

Another recent development in the Baltic is the stationing there of six Soviet Golf-class submarines, each carrying three SSN-5 missiles with a 750-mile range. (Later reports indicate that the submarines are actually launching platforms and are armed with SS-20 missiles.) The submarines use the Latvian port of Liepaja as their base and conduct routine patrols along the Soviet and Swedish coasts in a triangular formation, one corner of which touches Bornholm. Since Russian submarines in the Barents Sea can deliver nuclear strikes against northern and Western European cities, the Baltic-based submarines are probably intended chiefly for intimidation—although they obviously bolster the Warsaw Pact's theater nuclear strike force. When the submarines (which are diesel-powered and were built around 1960) first appeared in the Baltic in 1976, littoral countries assumed that they were on temporary maneuvers or were en route to nearby repair facilities. When it became clear that they were permanent launching platforms for atomic warheads, both NATO and Swedish officials protested. The Swedes cited Soviet hypocrisy in deploying such weapons in an area that Moscow advocates as a "sea of peace and cooperation." Sweden, which favors Finnish proposals for a nuclear-free zone in northern Europe, also castigated the USSR for moving nuclear arms ever closer to Scandinavia.[31] On Novem-

---

[31] Some military analysts speculate that the submarines were transferred from the Kola Peninsula to the Baltic because of overcrowded conditions. They contend that dispatching the subs to the Baltic Fleet is in line with the Soviet practice of maintaining obsolescent weapons systems rather than scrapping them as the Americans do. Such an explanation, however, hardly accords with Moscow's failure to inform any of the Baltic countries that the submarines

ber 1, 1978, the new Swedish foreign minister, Hans Blix, proposed inclusion of the Baltic in a nuclear-free area in the north.

Soviet pressure in the western Baltic is mounting not only from the sea but also from the air. Warsaw Pact naval exercises in both the Baltic and the North Sea have been accompanied by flights of long-range bombers. As John Erickson describes it, "Soviet air activity results in the commitment of flights of strike bombers to within minutes of Danish airspace, turning what was an abnormal alert situation into a regular occurrence and thus straining the Danish military alert system."[32] Another observer says: "Since 1970 Soviet aircraft have been flying reconnaissance missions from the east to Cape Arkona and the island of Rügen.... From there they turned south over East German territory. Lately, however, they have been turning north instead to reach a position west of Bornholm...."[33] There has also been an increase in Soviet reconnaissance flights by 2,000-mph MiG-25 Foxbat interceptors based in Poland. Three new Soviet airbases have recently been built in Poland. The stationing on Polish soil of the Backfire, the Su-19 Fencer, and the MiG-23, along with the Foxbat and Soviet Naval Air Force units, reflects a clear expansion of offensive air capability. Also ready for use in the Baltic theater is the Hind-D helicopter, which is designed to carry assault troops and to perform antitank operations.

Soviet Military Diplomacy and Espionage on the Northern Flank

Accompanying the Communist military buildup in both "theaters" of NATO's northern flank has been a degradation of the USSR's diplomatic language vis-a-vis the Nordic coun-

---

would be deployed and with its sharp criticism of Western officials who said the boats were nuclear-armed. The submarines fit much more readily into the pattern of armed coercion aimed at neutralizing the northern flank.

[32] Erickson, "The Northern Theater," p. 10.

[33] *Manchester Guardian Weekly,* March 6, 1977.

tries. The Soviet attitude here, as elsewhere, appears to be that the shift in the "correlation of forces" in favor of Communism gives those countries no alternative to détente—on Soviet terms. The term "military diplomacy" (which has been used in a different context to connote surrogate military force in the service of Soviet diplomatic goals in the Third World) is used here to refer to Moscow's manipulation of its regional military superiority to dictate to the northern flank countries on political matters. Analysts have referred to this situation variously as "armed coercion" or establishment of a "special atmosphere" in which Soviet wishes will be respected by reflex in the Nordic states. Sufficient Soviet political and psychological leverage along the northern flank would permit Moscow to dominate the region without resorting to war.

A virtually unprecedented display of Soviet diplomatic arrogance toward Norway occurred during a meeting in December 1977 of Nordic prime ministers in Helsinki. Kosygin warned the Norwegians to desist from unspecified "provocations" along the Soviet frontier and in the Baltic. His displeasure was said to be motivated primarily by plans for a 1,500-man West German contingent to participate in NATO maneuvers in northern Norway. At Moscow's evident behest, the East German military journal *Die Volksarmee* added its voice to this controversy. In an article on January 11, 1978 the journal wrote that "Norway has developed into a platform for preparations for military aggression. The country is being increasingly drawn into a military strategy which threatens its national interests." Aside from "provocative" West German troop maneuvers, said the article, "West German fighters are temporarily stationed at Norwegian supply bases. This practice is undermining Norway's stated policy of not allowing foreign troops to be stationed on Norwegian territory." This typical Communist propaganda barrage, combining threats with alleged regard for "national interests," has also been aimed against the Danes whenever they appeared to be taking a more active role within NATO.

Kosygin's outburst drew sharp criticism from virtually all the participants at the Nordic conference. Norway's *Aftenpos-*

ten editorialized on December 10, 1977 that while "allegations" regarding Norwegian defense policy had appeared in Soviet media, "when they are made by the head of government at a personal meeting with his Nordic counterparts, they must be taken more seriously. There is little reason to believe that it was a sudden impulse which made Kosygin launch into a 'battle royal' with Scandinavia. It's more probable that Kosygin deliberately intended using this opportunity mainly to 'read the riot act' to the Norwegian and Danish prime ministers about their countries' NATO membership." *Aftenposten* added, "At times it can appear that relations between Oslo and Moscow are becoming warmer than is actually so. But Premier Kosygin's attack . . . is a reminder that it is dangerous to indulge in illusions." An editorial on the same day in the Copenhagen newspaper *Berlingske Tidende* declared that Kosygin raised questions "in a way which particularly implied very distinct criticism of Norway's NATO policy. This is in absolute contrast to the low profile which has marked Soviet policy toward Scandinavia as a whole for many years."

The reaction from neutral Sweden was particularly noteworthy. On December 11 a Swedish commentator stated that

> some people interpret the discussion by saying that Kosygin acted as if he were in another circle—the Warsaw Pact countries, where East European brother countries have to put up with the rebukes of big brother, the Soviet Union. This time the Nordic countries were involved, but Kosygin nevertheless took the opportunity to act like a schoolmaster. . . . First, Norwegian Prime Minister Nordli had trouble with Kosygin, who criticized Norway's military cooperation with West Germany within NATO. This irritated Danish Prime Minister [Anker] Jorgensen, who started to defend Nordli and referred to the increasing naval presence and insolence of the Warsaw Pact countries in the Baltic. The result was that Kosygin gave a talking-to to Jorgensen.
>
> It's . . . clear that the Soviet criticism is especially aimed

at Norway. Conservative newspapers in Norway have already interpreted the Helsinki incident as a Soviet attempt to frighten or at least soften Norway before the forthcoming extremely important talks about the division of the continental shelf in the Barents Sea.

Shortly after Kosygin's lecture, Soviet party chief Leonid Brezhnev sent the Nordic chiefs of state—and leaders of most other Western countries—identical letters warning them to dissociate themselves from the production and deployment of the neutron bomb. *Berlingske Tidende* commented that

> Brezhnev's warning... is stated in a rough and unpleasant manner.... The Nordic heads of government were subjected to [the Soviet campaign against the N-bomb] recently in Helsinki, when Premier Kosygin warned them against the neutron bomb in a very maladroit way.... The Danish government members have politely and on several occasions during bilateral talks referred to the insecurity caused by the East's military exercises and surveillance activity very close to Danish territory. In Helsinki, Kosygin brusquely told... Anker Jorgensen that he didn't want to discuss those sorts of details.

Strong Soviet diplomatic pressure has also been exerted against the northern flank countries on boundary questions. The most obvious example is the Soviet-Norwegian dispute over demarcation lines in the Barents Sea. Norway argues that the median line, equidistant from the two countries' borders and islands, should be the dividing line; but the USSR (citing the extraordinary military significance of the region) insists on the so-called sector principle, which would place the boundary along a straight line between the Soviet-Norwegian frontier and the North Pole and thus closer to Norway's coast. Norway also argues that the shallowness of the Barents Sea up to and beyond Svalbard makes that area one continuous continental shelf subject to Norwegian jurisdiction. The Soviet Union counters with the claim that Svalbard has its own shelf and that Norway should have sole access to offshore resources only within the four-mile territorial sea. The disputed waters in the Barents cover an area where oil and fish abound and where the USSR may want to establish a "sanctuary" for its SSBNs. Moscow seeks to exact Norwegian concessions in a bilateral forum that will create a pattern for future negotiations over northern issues. Bilateral arrangements in the Barents Sea involving the grant of special privileges to the Soviet Union would push Norway into conflicts with its own allies.[34]

The importance of border issues as a barometer of the Kremlin's evolving strategy for the northern flank has been aptly summed up in the following manner: "The Norwegian-Soviet boundary is part of that virtually sacrosanct set of boundaries on which East-West stability is built. A severe dispute relating to its extension into the ocean would thus be extremely unwelcome to both sides so long as current assumptions about détente remain valid. Should the Soviet Union wish to extend her influence more strongly into Scandinavia, however, such a dispute might serve her purposes."[35]

Other boundary issues have been manipulated (and, indeed, originated) by the USSR on the northern flank. The Soviet Union, for example, has refused to accept the median principle in the Baltic off the Swedish island of Gotland, and Poland has disputed the extent of Denmark's fishing zone off Bornholm. Several other incidents have raised friction in the Baltic. In June 1976 East Germany tried to seize a Danish torpedo boat there. Shortly afterward, Soviet and East German ships attempted to disrupt a Danish naval exercise, prompting Denmark to announce that it was prepared to seal off Soviet bases

---

[34] Moscow's mounting pressure on Oslo to deal with problems bilaterally was most cogently illustrated during a visit to Norway by Soviet Deputy Foreign Minister Igor Zemskov. He raised the question of working out a political consultation agreement encompassing joint consultations whenever problems of mutual interest arise. He may have also proposed a periodic exchange of visits by high-ranking military officers and top officials of the Soviet and Norwegian defense ministries.

[35] Barry Buzan, "A Sea of Troubles? Sources of Dispute in the New Ocean Regime," *Adelphi Papers,* No. 143 (London: International Institute for Strategic Studies, Spring 1978), p. 24.

around Leningrad by mining the Baltic exits.[36] In March 1978 Swedish customs vessels forced two Soviet fishing trawlers into the port of Faaroesund in Gotland after they were discovered in a prohibited military zone. In April the crew of an East German fishing research vessel was arrested for photographing military installations in the town of Horten in southeastern Norway. In September, Denmark, in an effort to enforce new guidelines for foreign warships' passage and stay in Danish waters, forced three Soviet warships to leave Aalbeck Bay, where they were monitoring the NATO exercise "Northern Wedding." The guidelines stipulate that foreign military vessels can anchor in Danish waters only after obtaining special permission and in case of emergency. Warsaw Pact ships have long used the bay as an anchorage for their warships en route to and from the Baltic and have stationed a tanker there to refuel them. Now Denmark has extended her territorial waters three nautical miles east of a new line drawn from Skagen to the south; Aalbeck Bay lies within this territorial limit. The presence of the Soviet warships in the prohibited zone led not only to a confrontation with Danish naval vessels but also to a stiff protest note to the Soviet ambassador in Copenhagen.

If Soviet and Warsaw Pact espionage activities carried on under various pretexts have been somewhat curtailed at sea, they continue to thrive on land. The northern countries have so far remained helpless before a new instrument of snooping, as described in the *Times* of London on March 11, 1978:

> Heavy road transport vehicles filled with electronic equipment are being used by Warsaw Pact countries as a land equivalent to spy trawlers to collect intelligence information in Scandinavia. The spy vehicles travel regularly from the Soviet Union through Finland, Sweden and Denmark and then cross by ferry to East Germany. They carry the international TIR road haulage car net which permits them to pass without being examined by customs officials when they cross national boundaries. . . .

---

[36] *U.S. News & World Report,* August 16, 1976.

They are able to stop for a day or two at a parking site to trace military communications in the area without exciting suspicion. It is also relatively simple for them to have a breakdown or a rest at a roadside near military installations.

A network of transport companies established by the Russians throughout Western Europe in recent years assumes magnified importance when these enterprises are viewed as covers for the importation of espionage equipment and fronts for KGB operatives. It is especially noteworthy that the Transglobe Container Service (a subsidiary of the USSR's Transnautic shipping company), which is based in Hamburg, controls the movement of sealed container traffic throughout northern Europe.

KGB activities have been on the upswing in Scandinavia, as elsewhere. These activities include campaigns against Scandinavian intelligence agencies. They are modeled on the campaign of harassment against the CIA and may even draw their inspiration directly from American sources. "Dirty Work," a collection of essays edited by former CIA employee Philip Agee, includes a contribution by Swedish journalists Peter Bratt and Jan Guillou. Both served jail terms on espionage charges after they acquired and published material from an ex-agent of Sweden's military intelligence. Bratt and Guillou, whose contacts with KGB operatives in Stockholm were made public during their trial, contended that the country's intelligence service had collaborated with its U.S. and British counterparts, thus compromising Swedish neutrality. Meanwhile, in Denmark the publisher of an extreme rightwing magazine apparently cooperated with elements of the radical left to smear the reputation of the country's military intelligence apparatus.

In 1975 the Danes accused four KGB agents attached to the Soviet embassy in Copenhagen of industrial espionage among Danish subcontractors involved in NATO's F-16 aircraft project; the four were deported. In 1977 a clerk at the Norwegian Ministry of Foreign Affairs was arrested during a meeting with a high official of the Soviet embassy in Oslo. She reportedly confessed to a 30-year-long spy career with the USSR, during which time she transmitted "information of importance to Norway's security." The accused spy suffered a fatal heart attack while awaiting trial, but several Soviet personnel in Norway—including the head of KGB activities at the embassy—were expelled from the country.[37]

Aside from KGB and GRU (Soviet military intelligence) activities in the northern flank states, the Polish intelligence services focus special attention on Scandinavia. In addition, the East German city of Rostock houses a number of agencies and front organizations that promote subversion in northern Europe. On January 22, 1978, for example, Tass announced a meeting in Rostock of the standing committee of an international trade union forum for "the many-million-strong army of working people of Baltic countries, Norway and Iceland." Representatives of these countries voted to hold their 21st working conference in Leningrad under the motto "trade union cooperation in the struggle for peace, disarmament and social progress." East Germany also provides training in espionage and sabotage to Scandinavians recruited by the USSR. Soviet-bloc intelligence services in Scandinavia (as well as West Germany) frequently blackmail former Nazi collaborators into working for them by threatening to expose their past activity.

A new and particularly ominous form of Soviet subversion is the effort, spearheaded by the Soviet-controlled World Peace Council (WPC), to promote unionization of NATO armed forces and engage in pro-Communist indoctrination in the barracks. On March 17–18, 1979 the WPC sponsored a conference in Malmö, Sweden, reportedly to prepare for creation of a "soldiers' international." Delegates from soldiers' organizations in Sweden, Norway, Denmark, France, West Germany, the Netherlands, Belgium, Italy, Austria, Finland, Spain, and the U.S. forces in Germany attended; the latter three delegates represented illegal groups. The conference was

---

[37] See *Keesing's Contemporary Archives*, March 31, 1978, p. 28908.

originally scheduled for Copenhagen, but the Danish government banned it. Those attending were urged to spread the doctrines of Soviet-style peace and détente and thus to erode allegiance to NATO, particularly along the northern flank.

Finland as an Instrument of Soviet Policy on the Northern Flank

In addition to using the mailed fist of espionage and the velvet glove of détente, the USSR employs more indirect strategies as vehicles in its campaign to drive wedges between the northern flank countries and the rest of NATO. One such vehicle is Finland, which has increasingly projected Moscow's voice in circumstances where direct Soviet diplomatic pressure might prove counterproductive. In order to better appreciate Finland's indispensable role as a Kremlin spokesman, it is important to examine that country's political, economic, and military ties with the Soviet Union as they bear on developments and trends along the northern flank.

Finland's importance to the defense of the USSR—notably to the approaches to Leningrad—is such that Stalin was willing to sacrifice some 1.5 million Russian troops in the Finnish campaign. In addition, the late Otto Kuusinen, a native Finn, was the only foreigner ever to sit on the Politburo of the Communist Party of the Soviet Union. In 1948 the Soviet Union and Finland signed a Treaty of Friendship, Cooperation and Mutual Assistance. Soviet media claim that by entering into this treaty Finland became "the first Western country to take the road of détente."[38]

Finland is unique in having treaty relationships with the Council of Mutual Economic Assistance (CMEA) as well as the European Economic Community (EEC); both accords date from 1973. Current Finnish trade with the EEC (and with the European Free Trade Association [EFTA]) far exceeds the turnover with CMEA, but Finland is critically dependent

---
[38] *New York Times,* September 18, 1978.

upon Soviet supplies of energy (oil, gas, electricity, and coal), for which it need not pay in hard currency. [At the end of 1978 Moscow raised the price of oil for Finland by 14 percent, because of increasing difficulty in supplying its allies' petroleum needs.]

- Moscow and Helsinki recently concluded an accord for economic, technical, industrial, commercial, and scientific collaboration into the 1990s. According to a *Pravda* article of March 4, 1977, Soviet-Finnish relations aim "toward the formation of a new type of international division of labor in which states with different social systems would take part [in] the consolidation of new relations in the form of long-term agreements...." Soviet-Finnish collaboration on a wide variety of industrial projects in both countries has proceeded apace. Some of them are in areas of Karelia that previously belonged to Finland.

In March 1977 Kosygin journeyed to Finland, ostensibly to inaugurate the country's first atomic power plant, which was built with Soviet assistance, but in large measure to symbolize
- the expanding economic ties between the two nations. At a dinner given in his honor by Finnish President Urho K. Kekkonen, the Soviet premier declared that Soviet-Finnish relations "can be regarded as the forerunner of the relaxation of tension in Europe" and as a vivid example of the implementation of "the new interstate relations elaborated by V. I. Lenin." Kosygin added that "the 1948 treaty represents a lasting guarantee of Finland's independence and plays an important role in insuring the Soviet Union's security in the region of its northeastern borders. It reliably serves the preservation of peace and stability in northern Europe."[39] The joint com-
- muniqué issued at the end of Kosygin's four-day visit underlined the need for "strengthening peaceful relations in the north of the continent and the Baltic Sea basin."[40]

An excellent example of the scope of Soviet-Finnish economic collaboration can be seen in the joint construction of

---
[39] *Pravda,* March 23, 1977.
[40] Tass, March 26, 1977.

the Rautarruukki metallurgical combine in Raahe, a city in Finnish Karelia whose population has tripled since 1960. This enterprise will receive much of its raw materials from a mining and ore-enrichment complex in Kostomuksha, a tiny community in Soviet Karelia some 25 miles from the Soviet-Finnish frontier. The Finns are participating in the Kostomuksha project, which is designed to tap Karelia's valuable resources and to transform the local community into a sizable city for metalworkers, with easy access to other newly settled areas of the Soviet far north. A railroad running from Kostomuksha to Kontiomäki, in Finland, has greatly reduced the time needed to reach the ports on the Gulf of Bothnia. The military significance of this railway, as of the roadbuilding and much of the other economic infrastructure being laid in this strategic region, should not be overlooked. Kosygin and Kekkonen participated in the laying of the cornerstone of the Kostomuksha project in September 1978. Again, the political significance of Soviet-Finnish economic cooperation was emphasized in Soviet media.[41]

Many knowledgeable observers believe that the process of Finland's economic absorption by the USSR has advanced dangerously far. In view of the Soviet Union's concentrated buildup of its northern regions as a zone for defense-in-depth of vital Soviet bases, this economic trend has definite military implications. Particularly intriguing in this context are Finnish proposals for cooperation among Norway, Sweden, Finland, and the USSR in the development of the North Cap region of the Arctic. Helsinki views this area as encompassing the northern zones of the three Scandinavian nations, as well as the Kola Peninsula and Pechenga. The Norwegians and Swedes have been notably unenthusiastic about Finland's ambitious plans for the North Cap—and doubly so when a Russian role in the scheme is mentioned.

Soviet-Finnish military coordination may also have ad-

---

[41] Ironically, the Finns used to dream of incorporating all of Karelia into a Greater Finland. Now the Russians may be contemplating an incorporation in reverse.

vanced further than is generally recognized. Conservative circles in Scandinavia reportedly believe that "the Soviet Union may be using Finland as a Trojan horse in order to upset the strategic balance in the North."[42]

Finland, whose armed forces are supplied in part by Western countries, seems locked in a struggle against lengthening odds to preserve a credible neutrality without provoking the USSR across the 900 mile-long, virtually indefensible border. Soviet pressure mounted during a summer visit to Helsinki by Defense Minister Dimitri Ustinov, who reportedly urged joint army maneuvers. Soon after Ustinov's departure, *Tiedonantaja*, the newspaper of the pro-Moscow faction of the Finnish Communist Party, printed several editorials urging the government to institute "joint Finnish-Soviet military maneuvers of some degree" and charging that Finland's neutralism played into the hands of NATO.[43] The issue was apparently raised again during Kekkonen's trip to Moscow in September, but he is said to have resisted maneuvers. Oslo believes that the Russians might have tried to link the maneuver request to a demand that Norway abandon its plans to deploy NATO equipment in its northern provinces for use in the event of a Soviet military incursion there. *Tiedonantaja's* editor later "explained" that his calls for maneuvers should not have been interpreted as recommendations for "shooting or practicing the arts of war" with the Russians.[44]

Nevertheless, the outcome of Kekkonen's visit remains unclear—and thus unsettling to Norway and the rest of the northern flank. The 1948 Soviet-Finnish treaty stipulates that Finland will repulse all military action against the USSR across Finnish soil by Germany or its allies and that the signatories will hold consultations in case of a threat of such attack. What the pact entails for Finland in strictly military terms has never been spelled out. Under these circumstances, a report

---

[42] F. B. Singleton, "Finland Between East and West," *World Today,* August 1978, p. 328.
[43] See the *New York Times,* November 15, 1978, and *Frankfurter Allgemeine Zeitung,* September 16, 1978.
[44] *New York Times,* November 15, 1978.

on the Swedish radio on September 23, 1978, shortly after Kekkonen left the USSR, takes on added import: "Nobody knows what was really discussed, but on [Kekkonen's] return there was vague talk about the trip being one of the most important ever, that it had yielded unusually fruitful results, and since Kekkonen on previous occasions has opposed an interpretation of the pact as linking Finland totally militarily to the Soviet Union, it is not unreasonable to assume that it was precisely the matter of military cooperation that he raised in the Soviet Union, although this cannot be officially confirmed...." It is noteworthy, however, that General Lauri Sutela, Finland's Commander-in-Chief, was "vacationing" in the Soviet Union at the same time as Kekkonen was visiting. According to a September 20 article in *Krasnaya Zvezda*, the organ of the Soviet armed forces, Sutela and Marshal Nikolai V. Ogarkov (Soviet first deputy minister of the defense and chief of the general staff) initialed a program for military cooperation through 1979 providing for "exchange of visits by military leaders and ships, air forces, air force sub-units, delegations from military training establishments, and other corresponding measures." According to at least one analyst, "This appears to portend successful culmination of a Soviet effort, which Finnish military leaders long sought to evade, to bring Finland's armed forces into close coordination with the USSR's."[45]

The issue of closer Soviet-Finnish military cooperation must be viewed against the background of a controversial book published in the Soviet Union in 1976. Entitled "Thirty Years of Good-neighborly Relations" (*Tridtsat let dobrososedstva*), it was written by T. Bartenev and Yu. Komissarov, believed to be pseudonyms. The book, which may have been a trial balloon to test Finland's reaction to closer Soviet-Finnish

---

[45] Soviet World Outlook, October 15, 1978, p. 6. An article in *Krasnaya Zvezda* on March 15, 1977 may have presaged such coordination. A delegation from the military education establishment of the Soviet armed forces was reported to be in Finland at the invitation of the chief of the Finnish general staff to "familiarize itself with the Finnish defense forces, military educational establishments, and the officer cadre training system in the country."

military ties, implied that the 1948 treaty is a virtual mutual-defense pact and that Finnish neutrality would be almost impossible to sustain in an East-West conflict in which the treaty was invoked. In truth, the accord only requires the Finns to fight on their home territory against an invader and to consult with Moscow in the event of a threat of aggression against Finland or against the USSR across Finnish soil. Soviet military assistance is to be supplied only if there is "mutual agreement between the Contracting Parties."[46] Several Finnish media viewed the Bartenev-Komissarov treatise as psychological preparation for reducing the country to the status of a Soviet satellite.

In November 1978 the Finnish parliament authorized acceptance of a 50 million-ruble credit from the Soviet Union for military purchases. The unusual circumstances surrounding the transaction were outlined by *Aftenposten* on November 13:

> The explanation for entering into the agreement says only that the credits will be used to purchase "special material," which the Soviet Union will supply during 1979–80. It will consist of SAM-3 air defense missiles for defending Helsinki and new MiG-21 aircraft already ordered by Finland. These orders are in no way secret. The Soviet desire for Finnish discretion therefore seems remarkable.... In accordance with Soviet wishes, only members of the Parliamentary Foreign Committee have received confidential information on what the ruble credits will in fact be used for.

In the meantime, Helsinki has announced the biggest reorganization of the defense forces ever undertaken in peacetime. It includes creation of a jaeger brigade and other measures to

---

[46] See *Yearbook of Finnish Foreign Policy, 1976* (Helsinki: Finnish Institute of International Affairs, 1977), p. 22, and F. B. Singleton, "Finland Between East and West," p. 323.

bolster military strength in thinly populated Finnish Lappland.

In view of the continuing Soviet military buildup on the Kola Peninsula and Finland's strengthening of her own northern region, the Finnish proposal for a demilitarization of the Soviet-Norwegian frontier assumes special importance.[47] It is, however, merely the latest in a number of Finnish initiatives undertaken with Moscow's blessing with the aim of weakening NATO's position along the northern flank. One of the most durable of such initiatives is Kekkonen's proposal, first put forth in 1963, of a nuclear-free zone in northern Europe. Finland's chief motivation appeared to be foreclosure of a possible West German role in a NATO multilateral nuclear force (MLF). The West German connection has continued to figure in Helsinki's proposal, but now the Finns also seek to preclude changes in Norway's policy of forbidding Allied nuclear weapons on its territory. Since a nuclear-free Scandinavia would so greatly facilitate Soviet military operations out of Murmansk in case of war, it is difficult to avoid the impression that Kekkonen's proposal was hatched in the Kremlin. In 1975 the Geneva Disarmament Conference even created a working group under a Finnish chairman to study the feasibility of a nuclear-free zone in the north. During an interparliamentary conclave on European security in Belgrade that year, however, Finland's perennial proposal prompted the Swedish head of the meeting's security committee to ask the Soviet delegate whether the Kola Peninsula would be included in the nuclear-free zone.[48]

In a speech to the Swedish Institute of International Affairs on May 8, 1978, Kekkonen took his concept of a nuclear-free zone a step further by recommending that "the Nordic countries should in their own interest enter into negotiations among themselves and together with the great powers. . . . The objective would be a separate treaty arrangement covering the

---

[47] Kekkonen raised the issue of neutralizing the Finnish-Norwegian border as early as 1965.

[48] George Maude, "Finland's Security Policy," *World Today,* October 1975, p. 407.

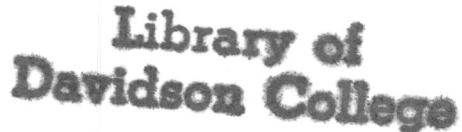

Nordic countries which would isolate them as completely as possible from the effects of nuclear strategy in general and new weapons technology in particular."⁴⁹ The Swedes, who, like the Norwegians, wish to retain their nuclear options, were presumably unimpressed. Norway's position has best been summarized as follows: "The official Norwegian position is clear: Northern Europe is already a nuclear-free zone, but creating a permanent obligation to keep it that way would deny Norway ... the right to summon nuclear forces in an emergency; it would thus restrict the room for maneuver in Norway's foreign policy, for the threat of changing her nuclear-free status may be considered ... an effective counter-thrust to rising Soviet pressure on any part of Northern Europe, including Finland...."⁵⁰

In addition to recommending neutralization of the Soviet-Norwegian border and peddling its proposal for a nuclear-free northern Europe, Finland has played upon Norway's memories of World War II to warn against West German participation in NATO activities on Norwegian territory. The USSR, of course, has traditionally sought to divide the West Germans from their NATO partners. In the so-called "Note Crisis" of 1961, Soviet Foreign Minister Andrei Gromyko handed a message to the Finnish ambassador in Moscow warning that West Germany's mounting influence within NATO, and especially among countries on the northern flank, was averse to Baltic security. Only with great difficulty did the Finns persuade the Kremlin to forego its demand for consultations under the terms of the 1948 treaty, which mentions Germany by name. More recently, Soviet diplomatic pressure via Finland reportedly caused the cancellation of participation by 1,500 West German troops in the NATO exercise "Arctic Express" on Norwegian soil. According to an article in *Aftenposten* on December 6, 1977, Finnish criticism of the planned German role "irritated broad circles in Norway" but could be

---

⁴⁹ Quoted in Singleton, "Finland Between East and West," p. 327.
⁵⁰ Maude, "Finland's Security Policy," p. 407.

excused because of the "special circumstances" governing Finland's foreign policy.

Moscow appears anxious to cement military and economic ties with Helsinki while Kekkonen—who is 78 years old and has been in power since 1956—remains at the helm. These plans may be complicated, however, by the outcome of the parliamentary election of March 1979. *Pravda* and *Izvestia* warned on the eve of the balloting that inclusion of the Conservative Party in the government would severely damage Soviet-Finnish political and economic relations. The Conservatives had been excluded from ruling coalitions for 13 years, during most of which time center-left combinations held power. The Social Democrats emerged from the recent elections with 52 seats (down from 54) in the 200-member parliament, but the Conservatives increased their representation from 35 to 45 seats, becoming the second largest party. The three centrist parties—Kekkonen's Center Party, the Liberals, and the Swedish People's Party—emerged with 51 seats altogether, compared with 59 in the outgoing parliament, and the Communist-dominated People's Democratic League (SKDL) received 35, a loss of 5. Thus, a reconstituted center-left coalition could command a parliamentary majority, but only at the cost of alienating the Conservative Party's numerous supporters. Finland's rightward shift came as the country was battling its worst economic recession since World War II and an unemployment rate of 8 percent.

The fact that Moscow's wishes had to be seriously taken into account in the formation of a new government attests to the extraordinary political influence wielded by the Soviet Union in Finnish internal affairs. The USSR's chief ally, aside from Kekkonen himself, is the SKDL, which participated in the previous coalition government with the Centrists, Social Democrats, and Liberals and belongs to the coalition formed in June 1979 with the Centrists, Social Democrats, and Swedish People's Party. This coalition, which excludes the victorious Conservatives, is headed by Social Democratic leader Mauno Koivisto.

The SKDL, headed by a non-Communist, includes the Finnish Communist Party (SKP), whose two wings are so deeply split that only pressure from Moscow has averted a formal schism. The majority wing, led by SKP Chairman Aarne Saarinen, advocates continued Communist participation in the government as an antidote to political isolation. On September 2, 1978, *Pravda* accused the *Kansan Uutiset,* joint organ of the Communist party and the SKDL, of propagating "Eurocommunism" and indirectly criticized the Finnish government for tolerating this heresy.

The minority faction of the SKP, under Vice-Chairman Taisto Sinisalo, adheres slavishly to Soviet policies but, ironically, has been unable to win Moscow's backing for its position that the Communists should shun participation in Finland's democratic process. The Sinisalo wing has steadily lost support in the trade union movement and other mass organizations, and in the March 1979 elections both Sinisalo and his heir-apparent, Markus Kainulainen, lost their parliamentary seats.

Domestic Underpinnings of Foreign and Defense Policies Along the Northern Flank

The Soviet Union, of course, does not call the domestic political tune in the other Scandinavian countries as it does in Finland. The Russians stand to benefit, however, from the breakdown of political consensus in these states. Since internal political configurations provide the undergirding for the foreign and defense policies of the nations along the northern flank, a brief glance at the domestic scene is necessary. Finland has already been examined; Norway, Denmark, and Iceland come next, followed by the special case of Sweden.

A general comment on political evolution within Scandinavia is apropos at this point. It can best be expressed in the words of a recent article in *The Nation:*

> Political turmoil has come to the region, and the consequences are serious. Sweden, Norway, Denmark, Iceland and Finland have been dominated for years by Social Democratic parties, governing alone or in coalition.

These parties tried to find, in Marquis Child's famous term, the "middle way" between capitalism and Socialism. Their promise of discovering the best of both worlds worked political miracles, bringing them a degree of consensus and unity that made them, for political scientists, models of political stability. But in the past five years the Social Democratic parties of these countries have found themselves in trouble, and as a result Scandinavia is at a political impasse not all that different from what has been plaguing the United States and Great Britain . . .

Rather than an end to Social Democracy, what we witness in Scandinavia is a stalemate, a situation in which the Left and Right parties in the Parliaments are splitting the seats fifty-fifty. But that in itself is significant, for a region that has prided itself on consensus is now bitterly divided along traditional Left-Right lines . . . [51]

Norway's Internal Scene

Growing political polarization in Norway has manifested itself particularly on foreign policy and defense issues. The country's tranquil political surface, long regarded as a barrier against Soviet penetration, was abruptly shattered over the issue of whether to join the EEC. More recently, the sharpest foreign policy debate in decades erupted in the *Storting* (parliament) over a new Soviet-Norwegian fishing accord covering the disputed "gray zone" in the Barents Sea. The controversy regarding economic resources-cum-defense in the Barents bears directly on the fundamental problem of formulating an appropriate response to the rising Soviet challenge to Norway.

The agreement, signed in Moscow on January 11, 1978, and ratified by a small majority of the *Storting* on March 9, created a temporary demarcation line between the 200 mile-wide exclusive economic and fishing zones off the countries' respective coastlines. Many Norwegian officials objected that, for

---

[51] Alan Wolfe, "The Stalemate in Scandinavia," October 21, 1978, p. 398.

the purposes of the treaty, the boundary line was drawn west of the median line that Norway seeks to establish in the final disposition of the issue. These objections were summed up by *Aftenposten* on March 8:

> [We are] left with a draft treaty which does not provide satisfactory guarantees against the fact that demarcation lines have in reality already been pushed further west than the point for which, in Norwegian opinion, there is justification in international legal practice.
>
> The incontrovertible result of the gray zone treaty is that the area of Soviet interest has been pushed west with Norway's blessing. We believe ... that it will prove particularly difficult to motivate Soviet negotiators to understand that in the next round we must again move the starting point for negotiations east of the demarcation line, which the Soviet Union consistently maintains is as far east as possible. The result is that Norway, by the agreement on the gray zones, has procured for itself a weakened starting point for the later and far more important negotiations on the final demarcation line between the countries' continental shelves.
>
> Not even as a fishing agreement is the temporary agreement satisfactory. The Soviet Union has gained a monopoly over 9,500 sq. km of sea area which, in accordance with the Geneva Convention [on the Law of the Sea], is Norwegian, while 10,000 sq. km becomes free water and 41,500 sq. km is included in the gray zone. The agreement is further hampered by the fact that 23,000 sq. km of undisputed Norwegian waters—waters which the Soviet Union has never doubted are Norwegian—are part of the gray zone. Throughout this area Soviet vessels can operate freely.... The agreement ... is not an acceptable solution for Norway, either in terms of fisheries or in terms of security and foreign policy....

To calm fears that the accord would set a precedent for final negotiating positions, a joint declaration was annexed to the document stipulating, *inter alia,* that the arrangements worked out in the temporary accord should not "in any way prejudice the position of the two parties."[52] Norway, however, takes the position that upcoming negotiations will apply to the demarcation of the entire economic zone, i.e., including the continental shelf in the Barents Sea, whereas the USSR contends that the joint declaration attached to the temporary accord refers only to fishing limits. Significantly, international law recognizes no difference between a demarcation line for a so-called "exclusive economic zone" and that for a continental shelf. Meanwhile, on June 15, 1977 Norway unilaterally established a 200 mile-wide fisheries protection zone around Svalbard's coasts and has sought to regulate the catch taken in that area by all the signatories of the 1920 Svalbard treaty. Strong Soviet opposition to this action has further strained overall Soviet-Norwegian relations.

Oil, which has already been discovered in large quantities under the Barents Sea and which may lie under the Kola Peninsula as well, is another issue roiling Soviet relations with Norway. Preliminary surveys indicate that oil reserves in the Barents Sea may be up to twice as large as proven North Sea reserves.[53] However, the difficulty and expense of extracting the oil, coupled with the Norwegians' ability to supply their petroleum needs for both domestic use and export from North Sea fields, render the oil issue less pressing. These economic factors have led Oslo to discourage oil drilling north of the 62nd parallel, which is the chief deployment and patrol area for Soviet SSBNs. Norway's ban on foreign oil-drilling in this area, however, is often perceived as another concession to Moscow's attempts to dictate developments in the strategically vital waters off Norway. Any move to accommodate the USSR on the Svalbard issue would be viewed similarly.

Many leftwing Norwegian politicians, however, favor closer

---

[52] *Keesing's Contemporary Archives,* March 31, 1978, p. 28907.
[53] See Myers, *North Atlantic Security,* p. 46.

cooperation with the Soviet Union; they believe such cooperation to be both necessary (in view of NATO's and the U.S. Navy's alleged inclination to abandon Norway in an emergency) and possible. They also contend that the Soviet military buildup on the Kola Peninsula is not an offensive move directed specifically against Norway but rather represents a bolstering of defenses for a possible East-West global war. They have been backed in this contention by statements from Undersecretary of Defense Johan Jorgen Holst. During a speech in Trondheim in January 1978, for instance, Holst declared that "paradoxically enough... the Kola Peninsula's significance and role in the balance between the great powers provides a certain insurance against an isolated attack [on Norway]. Such vital interests can only be jeopardized in extreme situations."[54]

Professional military men have deplored this opinion. As Colonel Terje Rollem wrote in *Aftenposten* on February 1, 1978:

> The great majority of our people want a defense which could prevent our country from being occupied. This means that the armed forces must be able to stop an aggressor until allied forces could come to our relief and continue the battle for us. Political circles have repeatedly stated that we have such a defense. This opinion is to a great extent not shared by the officers and NCO's who are responsible for waging the battle.
>
> The latest "confident" political assessment has been made by... Holst. He claims that a Soviet attack on Norway is made less likely because of the Kola Penin-

---

[54] Quoted in an *Aftenposten* editorial entitled "Norway and the Kola Base," February 1, 1978. During a visit to Moscow in February 1979, Holst told his hosts that "We... have in the formulation of our security policy placed weight on taking Soviet security interests into consideration at the same time as we naturally attend to our own... I can assure you that neither Norway nor our allies wish to turn Norwegian territory into an offensive threat against the Soviet Union." Quoted in *Arbeiderbladet,* February 15, 1979.

sula's strategic significance. Such a claim by the defense undersecretary can only be an excuse for a reduced defense effort. To the armed forces personnel, the claim sounds irresponsible and dangerous. It seems far more natural to assume that the Kola region's increasing significance could lead to the Russians being willing to take greater chances than previously with an isolated attack on Norway. Control over parts of northern Norway and Svalbard is a condition for the Russians to be able to wage war against NATO...

Another critical assessment of Holst's views came from Per Hysing-Dahl, chairman of the Storting's defense committee and a Conservative. Commenting on statements by Holst at a NATO meeting and on television that the Kola forces were mostly defensive and that the USSR was actually displaying restraint by limiting the buildup, Hysing-Dahl declared: "Of course... the Soviet force buildup on the Kola isn't primarily directed against Norway. But... it would be absolutely illogical if a superpower didn't order things so that in emergencies it could acquire a security area around this vital part of its military force... It's beyond doubt that the Soviet Union's military expansion is continuing. It's also clear that greater importance is now being attached to quality than to quantity...."[55]

Those who warn against minimizing the Soviet threat to Norway from Kola also criticize the Labor Party government for making too many unreciprocated concessions to the USSR. They point especially to the deviation from the median line concept in the temporary fisheries agreement, the alignment with Moscow's interpretation of the joint declaration regarding future negotiations on the "gray zone," the offer to give the Russians a "hearing" on Svalbard issues, and—perhaps most significantly—the modification of plans for West German participation in NATO exercises on Norwegian soil. The latter issue has had a peculiarly intense psychological ef-

---

[55] See the interview in *Aftenposten,* November 17, 1977.

fect in Norway, where latent fears of Germany remain and where many yearn for a return to the neutrality that was so rudely shattered by the Nazi invasion and that subsequently gave way to NATO membership. Soviet propaganda capitalizes on this psychological climate with a clever mixture of threats and cajolery. Deputy Foreign Minister Vasily V. Kuznetsov, for example, replied to an *Aftenposten* editorial on the growing Soviet threat to Scandinavia by stating that "Moscow wants to protect others from the 'adjustments' which the NATO staff and its branch in Bonn want to implement in the northern part of Europe. Such 'adjustments' can lead to undesired changes in the stable situation and the balance of interest in this area. And these 'adjustments' will not harm the Soviet Union ... but will harm the small countries, especially those which have tied their fate to NATO."[56]

Out of consideration for Norwegian public opinion, the government has traditionally prohibited West German participation in exercises held on Norway's territory by the Allied Mobile Force (AMF), which is designed to reinforce Norwegian units in war. The AMF "fire brigade" maneuvers are held in alternate years. In 1974 the Labor government of Trygve Bratteli decided to permit a German field hospital unit to join the 1976 exercises. In 1978 Prime Minister Odvar Nordli gave permission for a German communications unit and a helicopter contingent to participate as well. On January 19, 1978 *Aftenposten* reported that Oslo had informed a NATO summit in 1976 that West German ground troops would participate in future exercises in Norway on an equal footing with the other allies. According to *Aftenposten,* however, in January 1978 Soviet Deputy Foreign Minister Zemskov visited Norway for talks with Defense Minister Rolf Hansen and Undersecretary Holst. Soviet pressure, subsequently reinforced via Finland, led the Norwegians to renege on their decision. On January 9, shortly after Zemskov returned to Moscow, Holst announced that, instead of a 1,500-man contingent, only individual support sections of some 480 troops would represent West Ger-

---

[56] *Ibid.,* April 28, 1977.

many at "fire brigade" exercises. *Aftenposten* editorialized that "Norway is in fact accepting a Soviet claim that the memories of the war give the Kremlin the right to be heard when it objects to the West German presence in other parts of Europe. The government's latest decision also means a further limitation of Norwegian freedom of action and that a new restriction of our foreign policy is being introduced."

The Russian response to such Norwegian critics is typified by an article in *Sotsialisticheskaya Industriya* on October 3, 1978:

> ... the neighborly development of Soviet-Norwegian relations does not suit everyone. Certain influential circles in the country are seeking—with a persistence worthy of better application—the buildup of military preparations and increasingly active participation in NATO's so-called "northern strategy" that is acquiring a markedly nuclear flavor. Particular anxiety is being generated by the attempts of rightwing forces both within and outside the country to emasculate one of the basic elements of Norway's foreign policy course which, as is known, forbids peacetime deployment of foreign troops and nuclear weapons on Norwegian territory. In the front ranks of those who oppose these plans, which endanger the cause of peace in northern Europe, stand the Norwegian Community Party, the Norwegian Committee for Peace created in 1977 and other progressive organizations.

Although the Norwegian Communist Party (NKP) is a pliant instrument of Moscow, it provides a much less useful vehicle for Soviet influence over Norwegian politics than do the heated issues of economic resources-cum-defense off Norway's coasts that have created divisions both within and between the country's major political parties—the ruling Laborites and the opposition Conservatives.

The NKP's electoral strength has declined steadily from a high of 12 percent in 1945 (when the Communists, fresh from their role in the anti-Nazi resistance, briefly entered a coalition government) to 0.4 percent in 1977. Party membership numbers only a few thousand. In the late 1960s Chairman Reidar Larsen criticized the Soviet-sponsored invasion of Czechoslovakia and joined the ranks of "revisionist" Communist leaders and parties wanting to loosen their ties with the CPSU. His aim was to end the NKP's long political isolation by making it more responsive to local sentiments. Larsen's opportunity beckoned in 1972, when the Communists participated in the so-called "Red-Green Alliance" of leftwing Socialists, farmers, fishermen, and dissenters from the Labor Party to defeat the government in a nationwide referendum on Norwegian membership in the EEC. Several of these anti-Market groups decided in 1973 to create a loose Socialist Electoral Alliance (SV) to contest the parliamentary elections that year. Campaigning on an anti-NATO, anti-EEC, and strongly Socialist platform, the SV polled more than 11 percent of the votes and won 16 seats in the 155-member *Storting,* of which the Communists (namely Larsen) got one.[57] The Labor Party made its worst showing (35.5 percent) since the election of 1930 and became dependent on the SV for parliamentary support.

Soon afterward, the SV decided to transform itself into a genuine political party. Larsen canvassed Communist support to dissolve the NKP as a separate organization and merge it into the new party, but he met fierce opposition from pro-Moscow loyalists led by Martin Gunnar Knutsen. Despite disunity within Communist ranks, the components of the SV held a conference in March 1975 and passed a resolution reaffirming that the four separate groups would dissolve their organizations by the end of 1976. The new united body was to be called the Socialist Left Party.

Knutsen promptly told a journalist that the resolution on merger "means nothing to us" and called the new grouping "something halfway between a party and an electoral alliance." He added that "this halfway stage can go on as long as necessary" but that in the daily political struggle, the parties

---

[57] They obtained a second seat in 1975 after the death of an SV deputy.

inside SV [will] stand together."[58] Soviet reaction to the fast-breaking developments in Norway came in a *Pravda* article of March 25, 1975. Having reported an account by Tass of the Norwegian conclave, the newspaper commented that

> the SV conference has shown serious ideological and political differences of view among those parties and groupings constituting it. Having decided to establish a Socialist Left Party, the SV conference ... refused to include in the party program some ... fundamental principles of Marxism-Leninism, as proposed by the delegates of the Communist Party.... The continuation of the activity of the Communist Party of Norway on the basis of its established program ... preserves its ... significance from the point of view of the fundamental interests of the Norwegian working class [and] the struggle for peace, democracy and social progress.

In June 1975 Knutsen led an NKP delegation to Moscow, where he met with Mikhail Suslov, the CPSU's chief ideological watchdog, and Boris Ponomarëv, the Central Committee secretary in charge of relations with nonruling Communist parties. Larsen, ostensibly preoccupied with his parliamentary duties, remained at home. In a joint communiqué issued upon Knutsen's departure from the USSR and published in *Pravda* on July 2, the Norwegian comrade pledged that "the NKP would ... in the future be conducting its activity firmly on a Marxist-Leninist basis."

The local elections held in Norway in September 1975 went badly for the SV, whose image had been tarnished by the bickering among its component members—notably the Communists. Its loss of support, in turn, strengthened the hand of the Knutsen wing of the NKP, which had sharply opposed merger into the new Socialist Left Party. At the 15th NKP congress, in November 1975, Larsen was replaced as party chairman by Knutsen (Larsen later resigned from the party). The NKP's

---

[58] Quoted in *Aftenposten,* March 17, 1975.

new course leaves room for electoral cooperation with the SV, but the latter regards dual membership in the Socialist Left Party and another party as anathema. The NKP's dismal showing in the parliamentary elections of September 1977, in which it failed to win a single seat, reaffirmed the party's return to the political wilderness. It has been upstaged on the right by the Labor Party and the SV and has been chastised from the left by Maoists and other radicals that regard the NKP as the "left wing of the bourgeoisie."[59] None of this ill fortune has dimmed Knutsen's affection for Moscow, however. A statement by the Norwegian Communist boss that appeared in *Pravda* on February 22, 1977 retains validity:

> As far as our political line in general is concerned, it is clear. We want to find a path to Socialism while proceeding from Norwegian conditions and remaining totally loyal to the principles of proletarian internationalism.... Our party is endeavoring to offer active opposition to attempts to disunite the peoples and to sow mistrust among them, particularly in the form of anti-Communism and anti-Sovietism.... Such a policy is by no means... easy ... under the conditions of NATO in Norway. But the Norwegian Communists consistently advocate friendship with the Soviet Union....

If the Communist party appears as more of a liability than an asset in Moscow's drive to cultivate a new quisling, other trends within Norway may offer more promise. Despite (or perhaps because of) new oil discoveries, the country's economic situation is precarious. Technical problems, a major blowout, and other difficulties have kept petroleum production down. Oslo has amassed a foreign debt equivalent to $20 billion, borrowing against future oil revenues.[60] In February 1978 the krone was devalued by 8 percent, and in September

---

[59] Trond Gilberg, "Nordic Communism," *Problems of Communism*, May-June 1975, p. 31.
[60] See the *Wall Street Journal*, April 17, 1978.

the minority Labor government ordered a complete wage and price freeze to last until 1980, banned collective bargaining, and announced that there would be slashes in public spending. If unemployment on a politically significant scale results, Communist inroads into the trade union movement could increase. So far, the Norwegian Federation of Trade Unions has remained firmly under the Labor Party banner, and only among the longshoremen, construction, and transportation workers is there even a sizable Communist representation in the leadership of the locals.

Fresh difficulties could arise if Norway's NATO allies cite the country's newly discovered oil wealth to press Oslo into increasing the military budget and contributing greater financial resources to the alliance. Norway is already one of the few NATO members committed to a rising defense effort. In 1978 the Norwegian Defense Commission for the first time recommended a 15-year defense budget consisting of three consecutive five-year programs. It averaged 3 percent real growth overall. However, the government proposed only a 2.6 percent growth for 1979, despite NATO agreement for a 3 percent annual increase in real terms for each of the next five years. Norway cited current economic constraints but reassured her allies that the NATO target would be met in the overall five-year period.

In 1974 a Defense Review Commission was formed to examine Norway's long-term defense and security problems and to reaffirm a national consensus on foreign policy. The Commission, whose members represented the various political parties and influential bodies of opinion in the nation, generally sanctioned current defense policies.

Public opinion polls indicate that from 60 to 80 percent of the Norwegian people favor continued membership in NATO, but, as Holst notes, "Norway's membership ... has had the quality of a marriage of convenience rather than one based on passion." Moreover, "it is important to understand that the guarantee inherent in the alliance commitment has always been viewed primarily in *political* terms. It has constituted a long-term insurance policy against harassment, intimidation and attack."[61] Faced with Western inability to counteract Moscow's growing campaign of harassment and pressure, Norway may find that NATO membership yields diminishing returns and that the benefits of membership do not outweigh the risks. Already there exists a vociferous *Norge ut av NATO* (Norway Out of NATO) movement, as well as various groups calling for neutrality and peace and supporting other "progressive" causes.[62]

In addition, leftist politicians have frequently succeeded in embarrassing the Labor government or in bending its programs leftward. In 1977 two leftwing former members of the *Storting* published without authorization a report on establishment of a navigation station whose military use Norwegian and U.S. officials allegedly tried to conceal. In the fall of 1978 an editor for an Oslo publishing firm went on trial for compiling and circulating a list of monitoring stations operated for the United States by Norway and aimed at the USSR.

During a parliamentary debate on the 1978 budget, the entire Labor Youth Phalanx defied party discipline to vote for an SV proposal advocating Norway's withdrawal from NATO. Leftist deputies may also be able to block implementation of parts of the country's long-range defense program. The Socialist Left Party had an important role in extending new legislation on the 9-to-5 working day to the military and in passing laws that permit political activity among uniformed soldiers. Unions within the armed forces are now widespread and active. Conscripts' rights include periodic government-funded visits home from their remote posts in northern Norway. These visits not only divert military funds from defense-

---

[61] Johan Jørgen Holst, "Norwegian Security Policy: Options and Constraints," in J. J Holst, ed., *Five Roads to Nordic Security,* p. 79. Italics added.
[62] It should be noted that in both Norway and Denmark "the antiwar movements, the neutralist groups and the anti-Common Market forces have at all times been controlled by non-Communist elements, primarily the Social Democrats and the SF [Socialist People's] parties. . . . Indeed, the trade union leaders, who have provided a substantial amount of the money that the mass organizations have needed to operate, have emphatically insisted that Communist influence in these organizations be kept to a minimum." See Gilberg, "Nordic Communism," p. 31.

related uses but also affect the combat readiness of the units in the strategic and vulnerable North.

Socialist Left leaders recently threatened to publish lists of Norwegian foreign intelligence operations if an accused Soviet spy were brought to trial (this was the spy who died in pretrial custody). Ironically, this party, which refuses to label itself "Marxist-Leninist," may promote the Soviet cause in Norway more effectively than can the purist NKP. As a U.S. military analyst has noted:

> While the Norwegian Communist Party is aging ... and losing its influence, the non-Communist far left grows more vigorous. It draws much of its strength from the universities, intellectual associations, labor unions, young liberals and Socialists, and conscripts in the armed forces. It is from within these groups that one finds the inclination to question more closely the actions of the U.S. "ally" that those of the Soviet "enemy," and to permit the tar of U.S. identification with NATO to affect attitudes toward that organization. For example, the University of Tromsoe refused to admit an American scholar who had applied for study there on a NATO fellowship.[63]

The leftists even have their own policy research group—the Peace Research Institution of Oslo (PRIO)—which is funded by the ministry of education. PRIO, which during the early 1970s played a significant role in mobilizing opposition to Norwegian membership in the EEC, has more recently devoted attention to publicizing previously classified information regarding Norway's relationship with NATO.

It is clear in retrospect that the struggle over Common Market membership and the political coalitions it spawned had a decisive impact on the Norwegian democratic system. It hastened—and perhaps caused—the end of the Labor Party's

---

[63] Colonel Arthur E. Dewey, U.S.A., "The Nordic Balance," *Strategic Review*, Fall 1976, p. 55. The average age of NKP members is now 60. The party's traditional constituency has included industrial workers in Oslo and low-income groups in Finnmark and some other areas.

dominance and has constrained its freedom of maneuver on foreign and domestic issues alike. Persistent opposition to Norway's membership in NATO has led the government to tread gingerly on a whole range of defense issues—from review of the "base and ban" policy to fishing in the Barents Sea—for fear of reviving an anti-EEC type of coalition. Such caution maximizes the ability of Soviet propaganda to play upon conflicting opinions within the Norwegian body politic. Even more serious is the possibility that these domestic conflicts will stymie government action in the event of a military crisis. As Colonel Terje Rollem has written: "The really big question is . . . what will our authorities do if the Russians, for example, occupy Finnmark overnight and exert pressure to make our authorities accept this without summoning aid from NATO? As is known, NATO won't come unless the Norwegian Government requests it. We have now reached the point where this question hangs in the air here, among our allies, and certainly in the Soviet Union also . . . ."

Politics and Defense in Denmark

Denmark's shifting political currents have been reflected most dramatically in the rise of the Progress Party. Its leader is tax lawyer and political novice Mogens Glistrup, who made an international splash with his comment that Denmark's defense apparatus should be abolished and replaced by an automatic telephone service that would say "we surrender" (in Russian) to a would-be aggressor. The main thrust of Glistrup's party, however, has been a campaign for a significant reduction in taxes and a dismantling of much of the welfare state bureaucracy. With this platform, the Progress Party emerged as the second largest force in the *Folketing* (parliament), behind the Social Democrats, in the 1977 parliamentary election.

Political polarization was glaringly evident in the election, with the Right and Left dividing the vote almost equally. After complex maneuvering, the Social Democrats joined forces in August 1978 in a coalition government with the Liberals (who are in fact conservative). Social Democratic Prime Minister Anker Joergensen walks a delicate political tightrope: he must compete with the Progress Party for middle class support by combating inflation and reducing social spending and at the same time refrain from the type of austerity policies that would alienate the trade unions, which are the strongest pillar of Social Democratic strength. Meanwhile, there is sniping on the left—from the Socialist People's Party (founded by former Communist chief Aksel Larsen), the Left Socialists, and, of course, the Communists.

Like its Norwegian counterpart, the Communist Party of Denmark (DKP) reached its peak electoral strength in 1945, when the popularity it gained in the anti-Nazi resistance movement allowed it to join briefly a coalition government. In the most recent parliamentary elections, in February 1977, the DKP polled only 3.7 percent of the total vote and won 7 seats in the 179-member *Folketing*. There is another historical parallel with the NKP: Danish party chairman Aksel Larsen was expelled from the DKP in 1958 for "Titoist" tendencies, while Reidar Larsen of Norway was deposed for "Eurocommunist" inclinations.

Chairman Knud Jespersen, who died recently, declared in a *Pravda* interview of September 24, 1976 that "we are the revolutionary party of the Danish working class. Therefore, we've never been confined to the narrow framework of parliamentarianism." On the same day, Tass quoted CPSU Secretary Konstantin Chernenko, head of the Soviet delegation to the 1976 DKP congress, as praising the Danish party's loyalty "to the principles of proletarian internationalism." Under its new leadership, "loyalty to the Soviet party remains the sine qua non of DKP international activity."[64]

Most of the DKP's approximately 9,000 members come from the ranks of industrial workers and leftist intellectuals in Copenhagen. The party wields more influence in the trade

---

[64] *Yearbook on International Communist Affairs, 1977* (Stanford, California: Hoover Institution), p. 138.

movement than in electoral politics; a member of its executive committee, for example, heads the seamen's union. Denmark's Trade Union Confederation, however, is firmly controlled by the Social Democrats. The DPK's domestic program is reflected in the new party program adopted at the 1976 congress. It advocates, *inter alia,* public ownership of banks, heavy industry, and the energy sector. In foreign policy the Communists are particularly vociferous in denouncing Denmark's membership in NATO and the EEC.

The Communists seem to view their best opportunity for expanding influence in Denmark to rest in the country's dire economic straits. A long period of prosperity ended in the mid-1970s; the economy is now plagued by inflation, an 8 percent unemployment rate, a net foreign debt nearing $11 billion (about 20 percent of GDP), and a persistent $100 million current balance of payments deficit brought on largely by oil bills for a nation totally dependent for its energy needs on imports.[65] The coalition government's new economic program calls for a freeze on wages and profits and an increase in the value-added tax.

Soviet media sharply criticized the "deal" worked out by the Social Democrats and the Liberal Party as a scheme to thwart working-class demands for more employment and higher wages while kowtowing to big business and multinational corporations and allowing defense spending to rise under pressure from NATO. On December 14, 1977, for instance, *Sotsialisticheskaya Industriya* wrote that "the consequences of the arms race are being acutely felt in Denmark, in particular. Under NATO pressure, it is with tremendous difficulty that the country of 5 million people ekes out of its budget funds which are so essential . . . for other purposes and directs them toward arms."

On September 1, 1978 *Pravda* carried a long commentary on Denmark's internal scene under the title "A Burden on the Working People." It stated, *inter alia,* that the two-party coalition in Copenhagen is in itself a result of the crisis that has

---

[65] See the *Economist,* September 2, 1978, p. 45.

gripped Denmark in recent years. The country's economic and social problems ... are evidence of the failure of the calculations that some people linked with ... entry into the Common Market.... Membership ... has not alleviated but complicated Denmark's economic difficulties. The crisis phenomena are aggravated by the fact that its commitments to ... NATO ... are a crippling burden on Denmark. NATO's new programs for the arms race require a constant increase in military expenditure from its members. NATO's ruling circles are treating their junior partners in an increasingly cavalier fashion, demanding them to take part in a ruinous and senseless arms race....

DKP and Soviet propaganda have sympathized strongly with strikers protesting the new government's economic program. When shipbuilders walked out, Moscow noted that its orders for cargo and container vessels were an important source of job security for these workers.

In commenting on the 1977 Danish elections, *Pravda* noted on February 17 that the Social Democrats had increased their parliamentary deputies from 53 to 65 but that the "main bourgeois parties" (notably the Liberals) had lost seats and that "despite the frenzied anti-Communist campaign unleashed by rightist circles, the DKP retained its seven deputies." *Pravda* added that elections took place nearly every year in Denmark, a fact that "reflects the quickened pulse of Danish political life, which results from the difficulties in the domestic and particularly the economic situation." Much of the economic difficulty was said to stem from membership in the EEC.

Debate over the size of the defense budget has also drawn Soviet attention to Danish politics. The Defense Act of 1973 was supplemented by an accord among the major parties regarding a four-year budget frame. This was fixed at the price and wage level as of April 1, 1972, and was kept inflation-proof through the addition of annual sums in accord with the rise of prices and wages. The defense ministry won a hard-fought agreement for a 1.5 percent increase in the military budget in real terms in each of the following four years. Despite the vote at the 1978 NATO summit in Washington for a

3 percent annual boost in members' defense spending, the Danish government decided to adhere to the 1.5 percent figure for fear of reopening a Pandora's box.[66]

Denmark, like Norway, joined NATO reluctantly. The Danes would have preferred a Scandinavian defense alliance, for which abortive negotiations were held in 1948–49. Denmark, however, manifests less of the pervasive pacifism of Norway or Sweden, and the Danish armed forces are reputedly willing and able to fight alongside the Western alliance. According to a recent public opinion poll, about 60 percent of Denmark's population and 80 percent of its parliamentary deputies support Danish membership in NATO.[67] The Progress Party deputies are among those backing the alliance. Opposition to NATO in the *Folketing* is limited to some 20 members of the extreme leftwing parties (including the Communists) and to a few Radical Liberal and Social Democratic deputies.[68]

Denmark's strategic importance lies both in her role as a bridge between Norway and the NATO countries on the central front (notably Germany) and as the guardian of the Belts and Sounds leading from the Baltic to the North Sea and the Atlantic. The latter role also bolsters the defense of southern Norway, thus allowing Norwegian defense forces to concentrate on northern Norway. Like Norway, Denmark forbids nuclear weapons or allied troops to be stationed on her territory in peacetime. There have been rumblings of dissatisfaction with this policy, however, in the wake of increased Soviet military activity off the Danish coasts.

Overall relations between Copenhagen and Moscow have cooled since the signing in August 1975 of a ten-year accord on economic, industrial, scientific, and technical co-operation and the initialing in October 1976 of an agreement on political

---

[66] See *ibid.*, July 15, 1978.
[67] See Major John M. Flentje, "The Danish Defense Policy Process: A Brief Overview," Paper presented at the Annual Conference of the International Studies Association, Toronto, Canada, March 20–25, 1979, p. 17.
[68] *Ibid.*, p. 25.

consultation.[69] Recent irritants include Kosygin's scornful reply to Joergensen's concern over stepped-up Soviet naval and air activity in the Baltic; Moscow's red-carpet treatment of the visiting head of government of Denmark's Faeroe Islands in 1977; conclusion of a Soviet-Faeroese fishing accord; and Soviet propaganda attempts to exacerbate relations between Denmark and Greenland. As the parliamentary debate over home rule for Greenland proceeded (the measure was passed on November 17, 1978), Soviet media accused Denmark and her Common Market and NATO allies of plotting to exploit the island's oil, chrome, and other resources at the expense of the native Greenlanders.

Soviet naval activity off Greenland has increased in recent years, and scattered protests have erupted on the island against the NATO radar stations and other early-warning installations there. Most of the protests have apparently been spearheaded by young Greenlanders who were exposed to Danish radical leftists while receiving higher education in Denmark.

Danish radicals have been increasingly active in opposing Denmark's NATO membership. In April 1978, for example, leftist student protesters forced the NATO advisory group for aerospace research and development to shift the site of its meeting away from their campus in Aalborg. As in Norway, however, the neutralist, disarmament, and other anti-Western groups are under non-Communist leadership. They present less cause for anxiety than does the seemingly chronic instability of the Danish government itself.

Domestic and Foreign Policy Trends in Iceland

Interestingly, it was Iceland, rather than the "Eurocommunist" strongholds of Italy, France, and Spain, that most

---

[69] This agreement stipulates that either signatory may request joint consultations whenever problems of mutual concern arise. The USSR has sought a similar agreement with Norway.

recently admitted Communists into a Western European government. Much has been written about the Icelandic Communists (as about the Eurocommunists) as nationalists; but their brand of nationalism distinctly favors the USSR, insofar as they seek a disarmed (except for the coast guard) and neutral Iceland.

The Communist-dominated People's Alliance (PA), which has generally polled between 12 and 20 percent of the popular vote but reached a record high of 22.9 percent in 1978, is the chief electoral vehicle for the Communists. It has been described by the U.S. embassy in Rejkyavik as "the linear descendant" of the defunct Icelandic Communist Party.[70] In 1938 that party withdrew from the Comintern and eventually reconstituted itself as the Socialist Unity Party, which included leftwing Socialists as well as Communists. In 1962 Ludvik Josefsson, heading an independent majority of the party, beat back a leadership challenge from a vociferous pro-Soviet minority. In November 1968 the Communists formally dissolved their own party and announced the transformation of the PA, an electoral front that they had long dominated, into a "marxist political party."

One of the Socialist Unity Party's last acts was a ringing condemnation of the Soviet-led invasion of Czechoslovakia. On August 23, 1968 the party organ *Thjodviljinnn* editorialized that "the conduct of the leaders of the five Warsaw Pact countries has drawn a clear line between them on the one hand and all other Socialists in the world on the other hand." Subsequently, the party posed a resolution that "strictly prohibited any contact, association, collaboration or anything else of its members with any citizens of the Communist states which attacked Czechoslovakia."[71] Partly out of revulsion at the rape of Prague and partly in deference to Icelandic public opinion, the PA has indeed severed ties with the CPSU and remained aloof from international Communist gatherings. PA Chairman Ragnar Arnalds told an interviewer from the West German

---

[70] *New York Times*, December 1, 1978.
[71] *Morgunbladid*, Reykjavik, October 8, 1968.

newspaper *Die Welt* on December 27, 1973 that "we do not attend [West European Communist] conferences. This kind of meeting is not consonant with our type of party. Our framework is wider. For example, we have closer ties with the Danish and Norwegian Social Democrats than with the Communists in those countries. We also sent an observer to the Labour Party conference in Blackpool. Purely Communist conferences are not commensurate with our goals."

Relations with the independent-minded Yugoslav and Rumanian Communist parties are good, however, and Arnalds recently spent a week in Rome as the guest of the Italian Communist party.

The PA's 2,500 members come mostly from the ranks of trade unionists, radical teachers and students, diehard nationalists, and disenchanted former Social Democrats. In 1956–58 the Communists participated in a coalition government with the Social Democrats and from 1971 to 1974 with the Progressives. Neither of these coalitions lived out its full four-year parliamentary term. After a strong showing by leftist forces in the June 1978 elections to the *Althing* (parliament), Josefsson came within sight of the prime ministership. The elections can be seen as an Icelandic variation of the political polarization that has occurred recently throughout Scandinavia:

> During the postwar period, Iceland has been the one Nordic country in which the Socialists were much weaker politically than the Communists. As a result, there was nothing approaching a political dialogue between them, and when the People's Alliance entered coalition governments, the Socialists were left in opposition with the conservative Independence Party. The June elections, ending a center-right coalition, in which the Progressive Party was a junior partner under Independence Party leader Geir Hallgrimmsson, changed that picture. In a general shift to the left, the conservatives dropped from 25 seats to 20, and the centrists from 17 to 12—whereupon the Progressives said that they would not rejoin a coalition that was still numerically possible. On the left, the Peo-

ple's Alliance won 14 seats, a gain of 3. But the big winners were the Socialists who, from having only 5 seats, also went to 14. The fact that another small leftist party ... lost both of only two seats in the Althing accentuated the new division of the Icelandic Left between two roughly equal components, the reformist Communist and the traditionally anticommunist Socialists.[72]

More broadly, the *Althing* is divided almost equally between right and left forces: the combined total of the Independence and Progressive parties is 32 seats, as compared with a more lopsided 42 in the previous *Althing;* and that of the Social Democrats and PA is 28, as compared with 18 before. Thus, the new coalition government that was formed on August 31 may be unable to paper over the deep fissures among its component parts or to wield decisive influence in parliament, despite its formal two-thirds majority.

The PA, the Social Democrats, and the Progressives each have three cabinet seats, with the Communists holding the ministries of education and culture, industry, and trade. As a precondition of Communist entry into the government, Prime Minister Olafur Johannesson (a Progressive) and Foreign Minister Benedikt Gröndal (a Social Democrat) obliged the PA to agree to Iceland's continued membership in the Western alliance, to retention of the U.S.-manned NATO airbase at Keflavik, and to an austerity program (including a big devaluation of the krona) that would combat Iceland's runaway inflation.

Commenting on the election, Moscow noted that it

> ... greatly altered the country's political line-up, netting impressive gains to the opposition People's Alliance and Social Democratic working-class parties.... Although, unlike the People's Alliance, the Social Democrats did not call for a radical foreign policy program, the pledges

---

[72] Kevin Devlin, "No Communist Premier for Iceland," *Radio Free Europe Research,* August 25, 1978, p. 5.

> to improve the conditions of the working class brought the party a goodly number of ballots from voters dissatisfied with the previous government's domestic policies.... One exceedingly unpopular piece of legislation was the February 1978 antilabor act under which, among other things, pay rises envisaged by 1978 collective agreements to make up for the annual 30–40 percent inflation rate were to be reduced by half.... For the first time in 50 years, Reykjavik now has a City Council dominated by representatives of working-class parties.[73]

Another Soviet commentator observed that

> the [Icelandic] economy is in dire straits, the rate of inflation last year reached 45 percent, and the national debt is enormous. The wage-freeze law evoked the anger of the bulk of the population, who see it as an attempt by the government to shift the economic difficulties onto the shoulders of the working people.... The bourgeois government's pro-NATO foreign policy was not popular either. There is a powerful movement against the stationing of foreign bases on Iceland's territory and the country's participation in the North Atlantic bloc.
>
> Realizing that the events in the country were taking a turn unfavorable to the ruling coalition, the conservative forces unleashed a rabid anti-Soviet campaign in the press, hoping to drown out the criticism leveled against them with a clamor about a "threat from the East." Judging by the outcome of the election, this attempt did not yield the desired result.... Be that as it may, the new government will unquestionably have to heed the opinion of the majority of the Icelanders who are demanding better living conditions and a foreign policy based on cooperation and not on rivalry.[74]

---

[73] *New Times*, No. 35, August 1978, p. 16.
[74] *Ibid.*, No. 28, July 1978, p. 16.

The Keflavik base is a prime target of Soviet propaganda. Established in 1951 under a U.S.-Icelandic bilateral accord within the framework of the North Atlantic Treaty, it is a key installation for tracking Soviet submarines and aircraft in the North Atlantic and for maintaining NATO's air superiority over that ocean. Its facilities also include antiaircraft and antisubmarine weapon launchers and bunkers for warships. Keflavik's radar stations form part of the NORAD system that warns against nuclear attacks on North America. The base serves additionally as a refueling spot for U.S. military transport to northern Europe and would be an ideal rear base for aircraft involved in northern flank operations.

Increasing Soviet naval and air activity off Iceland led Washington to bolster its complement of fighter planes at Keflavik from 13 to 23 during 1978. Among the new additions were the first units of the Airborne Warning and Control System (AWACS) to be stationed outside the United States. The nine P-3 Orion antisubmarine planes and 12 F-43 Phantom fighter-bombers based at Keflavik reportedly intercepted about 150 Soviet military planes over the past year and escorted them out of the Icelandic Air Defense Zone.[75] There is an obvious parallel with the increased number of "scrambles" or alerts by Danish and Norwegian-based planes that are caused by intensification of Soviet air and naval forces in those areas.

The Keflavik base, coupled with the U.S.-maintained Keflavik airport serving the nation's commercial airline, is Iceland's second largest employer. Its closure would force a politically unacceptable number of Icelanders out of work. Nevertheless, the American Iceland Defense Force on the base (consisting of some 3,000 naval personnel, 1,000 air force pilots, and 120 Marines) stirs resentment in Iceland, which has no army of its own. In 1974 the government (of which the Communists were members) invoked the six-month period of joint negotiations that must precede a one-year notice of can-

---

[75] *Wall Street Journal,* June 21, 1978, and the *New York Times,* December 1, 1978.

cellation of the Keflavik accord. Subsequently, the United States signed a Memorandum of Understanding with Iceland that provided for retention of the base. PA leader Arnalds (who also serves as Iceland's minister of education) has reportedly won agreement from his coalition partners for creation in 1979 of a "committee for the study of security" that will be responsible to the prime minister rather than to the strongly pro-NATO foreign ministry and that will focus on the Keflavik base issue.[76]

Soviet propaganda on the base issue contains the same blend of threats and cajolery present in propaganda barrages aimed at Norway and Denmark: Iceland is warned about its continued ties to NATO while simultaneously being urged to follow its own national interests by treading a neutralist (read: pro-Soviet) path. In the meantime, Soviet-Icelandic trade, economic, and cultural ties are expanding. The Russian embassy is a third larger than any other diplomatic mission in Reykjavik and is reportedly headed by a senior official of the KGB. A five-year trade accord signed in 1975 provides for an exchange of fish products for Soviet raw materials and machinery. Iceland imports oil primarily from the USSR. In 1977 then Prime Minister Hallgrimmsson became the first Icelandic head of government to pay an official visit to the USSR. On September 28, while he was still in the country, *Pravda* praised the "established practice of holding Soviet-Icelandic consultations —in particular through the ministries of foreign affairs." The Russians have given such consultations high priority in their relations with all the Scandinavian nations.

The lack of formal ties between the PA and the CPSU should not obfuscate the fact that a Communist-led Iceland, both for geographical reasons and because of the narrow and fragile base of its fish-dominated economy, would soon find itself in the Soviet orbit. Moreover, Moscow differentiates clearly between party-to-party and state-to-state relations and exhibits no compunction about strengthening the latter even if the former are precarious. Certainly in the vital sphere of for-

---

[76] *New York Times,* December 1, 1978.

eign policy it is difficult to distinguish any serious divergence between the PA and the Kremlin. Thus, the apparent readiness of the U.S. State Department to accept with equanimity the possible elevation of Josefsson to the premiership was, at best, shortsighted.

The Special Case of Sweden

The political and economic uncertainties besetting Scandinavia in recent years seem to have hit Sweden with particular force. The Social Democratic Party, which formed the core of the government for more than three decades, lost the 1976 elections by a small margin. A nonsocialist coalition of the Center, Moderate, and Liberal parties assumed power under Prime Minister Thorbjorn Fälldin, a Centrist. Disagreements over the issue of nuclear power plants forced the coalition to resign in October 1978. It was succeeded by a minority Liberal Party government under Ola Ullsten.

Economically, Sweden, like Denmark, has moved from an era of prosperity to one of relative decline. While Denmark's largely agricultural economy and Common Market ties may serve as buffers against a crisis, however, Sweden is on its own internationally and relies upon its industries to generate the revenue necessary to maintain the welfare state. The shipbuilding, steel, iron ore, and, to a lesser extent, paper and pulp industries have all suffered in recent years because of competition from Asia and Latin America abroad and high costs and workers' benefits at home. The country has a large deficit in its balance of trade and payments and a foreign debt of some $7 billion.

Inevitably, Swedish defense calculations have been affected by the nation's economic difficulties. The traditional foreign policy of armed neutrality remains a sacred cow for all Swedish political parties, but the ability to pursue it successfully presupposes a strong economy. According to an article of November 1, 1978 in the Stockholm daily *Svenska Dagbladet,* Swedish defense expenditures for the coming fiscal year will climb 11.6 percent, but this figure does not compensate for price rises and inflation. Similarly, the military budget rose from $1.5 billion in fiscal 1973 to $2.95 billion in fiscal 1979, but the military share of the GNP decreased from 4.6 percent to 3.5 percent over that period.[77] Moreover, the air force has been halved in less than 15 years, and by 1983 a tank brigade, a naval attack flotilla, three frigate units, and four coastal artillery units will be disbanded, and air strike and reconnaissance squadrons will be reduced in number. The government hopes to balance this loss through the introduction of new weaponry: heavy, mobile coastal artillery; a third minelayer; Nacken A-14 submarines; a new missile for the army; domestically produced Viggen JA-37 aircraft; missile-armed patrol boats from Norway; and torpedo boat missiles from the United States. However, Defense Minister Eric Kronmark told *Svenska Dagbladet* on October 1, 1978 that "our combat organization is continuing to deteriorate. In some areas, we are near the threshold where our defense capability could be in doubt." Kronmark added that many Social Democrats want further reductions in defense spending.

Unionization of the military has also had a deleterious effect on defense expenditure. In fiscal 1978–79, for example, more than 70 percent of Swedish military outlays were allocated for military personnel costs.[78] Moreover, Swedish regular servicemen belong to trade unions, and the government recently approved this privilege for conscripts. Leftists are pressing for the creation of a recognized conscripts' trade union.

Swedish public opinion appears largely indifferent to defense matters in general and to the mounting Soviet threat in particular. The news media perpetuate this climate of opinion by emphasizing the themes of détente, disarmament, and the evolving new international economic order in their coverage

---

[77] Colonel William J. Taylor, Jr., "Swedish Decision-Making for 'Total Defense'; A Fighter Aircraft Controversy," Paper presented at the Annual Conference of the International Studies Association, Toronto, Canada, March 20–25, 1979, p. 38
[78] See *The Military Balance, 1978–1979,* p. 31.

of foreign affairs. With the exception of the conservative *Svenska Dagbladet,* Swedish newspapers and television tend to be disinterested in defense matters or skeptical of Sweden's ability to influence the decisions of the superpowers.

In 1977 the National Psychological Defense Planning Committee conducted a survey of Swedish attitudes on defense. Among the findings were that credence in the deterrent power of Sweden's armed forces dropped to 31 percent from 55 percent in 1974; that faith in the country's ability to keep out of a major European war decreased to 23 percent from 38 percent in 1965; that belief in Sweden's ability to defend itself diminished to 20 percent compared with 30 percent in 1975; and that public assessment of the very significance of military defense dropped to 54 percent from 64 percent in 1975. Thus:

> One concludes that the Swedish public is not well informed about defense matters; that they are not anti-defense or anti-military and are generally willing to support defense, but, at a time of high inflation, they are concerned about rising defense costs. There appears to be a growing public tendency to doubt the threat of war, to view the military as a necessary evil to be funded at lower levels, and to want the military to go do its thing without interfering excessively with the important business of the welfare state.[79]

The so-called theory of "marginal attack" also contributes to the downplaying of military matters. Swedish military strategists assume that

> ... a power which might threaten or even attack Sweden will always have a substantial part of its resources tied up for other purposes, for example to counter any expected or unexpected confrontation with the other superpower. Thus, only a marginal part of the military strength of a superpower could be used in an attack on Sweden....

---
[79] Taylor, "Swedish Decision-Making for 'Total Defense'," p. 30.

> Provided that the goal in Sweden is limited and the country can defend itself, the value of controlling Sweden or part of Sweden will not be worth the cost of conquest.[80]

Interestingly, the credibility of this theory depends upon the extent to which NATO reinforcement of the northern flank will divert a Soviet concentration of strength against Sweden.

A comprehensive debate on the state of the Swedish armed forces is now in progress in the Defense Committee of the *Riksdag* (parliament). According to committee chairman Gunnar Nordbeck, "We'll go with seven or eight different attack scenarios, from a major war in Europe to an isolated attack against Sweden, together with peacetime crises." Among other topics to be examined by the committee is the consequences for Sweden of the Soviet military buildup on the Kola Peninsula.[81]

As early as 1975, Finnish media reported that Sweden's foreign minister believed it necessary to cooperate with NATO in weapons technology.[82] Sweden also sought to sell her Viggen fighter aircraft to NATO, but qualms as to whether Stockholm might withhold spare parts in order to uphold Swedish neutrality in the event of an East-West crisis led Norway and others to reject the planes. Meanwhile, Sweden's sharing of military-related industrial know-how with Norway and Denmark—and thus indirectly with NATO—has led to talk of coproduction schemes in weaponry. An extensive network of subcontracting across Scandinavian borders already exists. Sweden also purchases Western technology in the form of contract licenses for major components of its weapons systems. The Viggen JA-37, for example, is powered by a U.S. Pratt & Whitney engine manufactured under license by Volvo Flygmotor.

Moscow has seized on evidence of Swedish military modernization—as well as reports, denied by Stockholm, that the

---
[80] Nils Andrén *et al., The Future of the Nordic Balance* (Stockholm: Ministry of Defense, 1977), p. 85.
[81] See *Dagens Nyheter*, Stockholm, September 18, 1978.
[82] Maude, "Finland's Security Policy," p. 412.

Swedes considered equipping their forces with "mini-nukes" — to lambast Sweden for imperiling détente. The Kremlin was also annoyed by official Swedish criticism of the six Golf-class submarines in the Baltic. Reports that Sweden was seeking closer cooperation with the EEC have likewise drawn harsh Soviet criticism. A typical Soviet comment appeared in *New Times* on January 1, 1978: "How far is the present bourgeois government in Sweden likely to go in its desire to expand ties with the European Economic Community? This question is increasingly worrying democratic opinion in the country.... The Swedish press has reported unusually frequent visits by Swedish officials, industrialists and bankers to the Common Market headquarters in Brussels.... And the London *Guardian* reported ... that secret talks were underway between the Common Market and Norway and Sweden."

Sweden was a recipient of the letter sent by Brezhnev to various heads of government warning them to dissociate themselves from the neutron bomb. At the same time, the USSR has viewed Sweden's stance in favor of disarmament as helpful to its own propaganda offensive on this subject. When Social Democratic Premier Olof Palme was in power and the anti-Vietnam war movement was at its peak, the Soviet Union welcomed the voluminous anti-American rhetoric of the Swedes as a respectable vehicle of the Communists' global campaign against U.S. "imperialism." The USSR has also used Sweden (although to a lesser extent than Finland) in trying to "persuade" Norway to loosen its ties with NATO for the sake of Nordic peace and neutrality.

Sweden's nonsocialist governments have all but abandoned anti-American rhetoric, but they seek continued friendship and cooperation with the Soviet Union. In 1975 a ten-year Soviet-Swedish accord on industrial, economic, technical, scientific, and cultural cooperation was signed. Contracts have been negotiated for the enrichment of Swedish uranium in the USSR. In December 1977 the two countries concluded a fishing agreement. Sweden's state-owned Götaverken Arendal shipyard signed a contract with the Russians in April 1978 to build the world's largest floating drydock, which will be situated in Murmansk. Another Swedish firm is building a new air traffic control center at Moscow's Vnukovo airport. Former Foreign Minister Karin Soder apparently persuaded the U.S. Department of Commerce to permit the export of integrated circuits (which have military value) for this project.[83] Still another recent development involves creation of a joint Soviet-Swedish shipping organization called Scansov Transport AB. Its network of offices in Swedish ports is partly staffed by Russians—with obvious security implications.

As a symbol of friendship and good-neighborly ties, Swedish King Carl XVI Gustaf and Queen Silvia made a state visit to Moscow in June 1978. More significant, however, was the official visit to Sweden in September of Admiral Sergei Gorshkov, commander-in-chief of the Soviet Navy. Arriving at the invitation of Vice Admiral B. Lundvall, commander of the Swedish Navy, Gorshkov visited a naval base, naval college, and electronics plant; boarded a submarine and destroyer; received a briefing on the organization and training of Sweden's navy; and met with the Swedish defense minister, commander of the Swedish armed forces, and other military officials.[84]

Soviet propaganda claims that Sweden's economic downturn has intensified since the Socialists were ousted from power and that, despite election results, leftist strength remains formidable. The Russians clearly hope for a return to power by the Social Democrats in 1979. Certainly Palme's party, with its mass base, could be a more useful vehicle for Soviet policy in Sweden than could the small, sectarian Swedish Workers' Party-Communists (APK).

The APK represents the coalescence of three pro-Soviet factions of the Swedish Left Party-Communists (VPK) that split off from the parent body in 1977 after years of intraparty strife. Under C. H. Hermansson and his successor, Lars Werner (the current chairman), the VPK adopted a "Eurocom-

---

[83] See *Business Week,* August 8, 1977.
[84] Radio Moscow in Swedish to Sweden, September 14, 1978, and Tass dispatch from Stockholm, September 16, 1978.

munist" policy emphasizing a commitment to parliamentary democracy and relative independence of the Soviet Union. Pro-Moscow stalwarts within the party viewed this policy as an abandonment of Marxism-Leninism in favor of social democracy.

Although the Soviet Union strongly supports the APK, it maintains links of communication with the 15,000-member VPK. Indeed, there is nothing objectionable to the Kremlin in the VPK's program, which advocates, *inter alia,* soak-the-rich taxes, nationalization of banks and heavy industry, "an active struggle against big international monopolies," a six-hour workday by 1980, "a determined fight to reduce military expenditure and other costly, useless and unproductive activities," a new defense force of local "guerrilla units," and the scrapping of Sweden's new JA-37 Viggen aircraft.[85]

The VPK has expressed interest in formulating a joint program with the Social Democrats to be implemented in the wake of a Socialist electoral victory. Neither side indicates a desire for an electoral front, however. In the 1976 elections, the still-united Communist party won 4.7 percent of the vote and 17 parliamentary seats. Under Swedish law, the VPK, like all other parties, will have to poll at least 4 percent of the vote in 1979 in order to obtain parliamentary representation. The party's chief base is among the industrial workers of Stockholm and Göteborg, but the Social Democrats command the allegiance of the great majority of Sweden's working class and firmly control all trade unions at the national level.

During the late 1960s and early 1970s, the Swedish Communists played a political role greatly disproportionate to their representation in the *Riksdag*. Palme even named some Communists to the important legislative committees on defense and taxes until conservative party leaders protested. It seems that the most the VPK can look forward to in the foreseeable future is a resumption of a role as unofficial junior partner of a resurgent Social Democratic Party. The APK, for its part, may well be consigned to political oblivion. It is al-

---

[85] See *Yearbook on International Communist Affairs, 1977,* p. 231.

ready challenged from the left by such radical groups as the Communist Association of Marxist-Leninist Revolutionaries. According to an authoritative source, this group "has been riddled by internal conflicts, but it is a well-organized cadre party claiming 'cells' within Swedish industry and in the defense forces."[86] The Swedish Soldiers' Working Group, which is dominated by Trotskyites and Maoists, is also reportedly gaining adherents.

One reason for the split in the Swedish Communist Party was the ouster of the Socialist government, an occurrence that permitted the Stalinist factions to parade their contempt for parliamentary democracy without sacrificing the political influence that had been theirs under the Palme government. Thus, a return of the Social Democrats to power could precipitate a reunion of the feuding Communists, especially if the Socialists' majority is sufficiently small to require Communist support in the *Riksdag*. Reunion is unlikely, however, and certainly matters much less to the Soviet Union than does the extremely important issue of Sweden's continued neutrality in military matters.

It is noteworthy that Soviet military writings define NATO's northern flank as encompassing not only Norway, Denmark, and northern Germany, but also contiguous areas *(primykayushchie nemu raiony)*.[87] Sweden, with its geographical proximity, network of modern airfields, and modern weaponry, is preeminent among these areas. Its adherence to the Western side in wartime would severely complicate Soviet operations, both offensive and defensive. In particular, Sweden's neutrality would be a vital precondition for Soviet success in forcing the Baltic exits. At the same time, Sweden's defense policy is predicated upon the continued alherence of Norway and Denmark to NATO and the maintenance of overall stability on the northern flank.

---

[86] *Ibid.*, p. 233.
[87] See, e.g., Lt. Colonel V. Nikolayev, "Severnyi flang NATO," *Vestnik protivovozdushnoi oborony,* No. 1, 1976, p. 76–79.

The Nordic Balance, the Northern Flank, and Soviet Policy

A vague concept of Scandinavian unity, as portrayed in the notion of a Nordic balance, has often been cited as a deterrent to Sovietization of the region. The image is one of a scale, with neutral Sweden holding the balance between pro-Western Norway, Denmark, and Iceland on the one side and Finland, whose foreign policy operates under Soviet sufferance, on the other. There is a tacit self-adjusting mechanism: for example, if Soviet pressure on Finland intensifies, the NATO presence in Norway and Denmark will increase. The theoretical equilibrium has vanished in practice, however. As a U.S. military analyst observes:

> To begin with, the force increase envisaged to offset the "base and ban" concession [no allied bases or nuclear weapons on Norwegian territory in peacetime] has yet to materialize in Norway. In the years . . . since the Storting unanimously recognized the need for the offset, there has been no serious attempt to bring it about. Yet the assurance, or self-restraint, stabilizer, which included not only "base and ban" but also bars to allied maneuvers in Finnmark . . . and allied air or naval activity east of 24°E. longitude, appears to be locked in concrete. Both within Norway and by the USSR, self-restraint as defined by these restrictions is viewed not as part of an adjusting mechanism but as a sacrosanct tenet of Norwegian . . . policy. For example, the Soviet side of the scales can be weighted at will with almost no likelihood of counterweights being added by the countries on the other side in the region (and, conversely, Norwegian attempts to strengthen its forces can be challenged by the USSR through invocation of its meaning of the "balance"). So one needs to view the Nordic Balance, not in terms of its potential as a stabilizer for the region, but in terms of the

dangers it holds, as currently practiced, for institutionalizing disequilibrium.[88]

The most significant shift in the balance from NATO's side would be abandonment by Norway and Denmark of "base and ban," but the domestic political repercussions of such a move make it extremely unlikely. In fact, Norwegian defense planners tend to view prestocking, or prepositioning, of equipment for NATO use as supporting the no-base policy.

The shifting of the Nordic Balance must be seen in the context of a tilt in the global "correlation of forces" in favor of the Communist bloc. Soviet propaganda beamed at the northern flank, as elsewhere, portrays the United States as having been dragged reluctantly into détente as the growing might of the USSR and the Socialist camp renders "imperialist" attempts to unleash war increasingly risky. Soviet media strongly imply that the shifting balance of forces may leave the United States both unable and unwilling to defend its allies—even those in NATO—for fear of bringing on a Soviet nuclear strike against the American homeland.

Washington has played directly into Moscow's hands in furthering the perception that its NATO allies might prove expendable in a crunch. By weakening its own defenses both via the Strategic Arms Limitation Talks (SALT) and through unilateral measures, the United States conveys the impression that it may have to acquiesce in piecemeal surrender in Europe (witness published reports that U.S. officials are resigned to the loss of one-third of West Germany in the initial stages of a European war)—and may, indeed, prove helpless against the blitzkrieg that Soviet military doctrine advocates. Thus, the Carter Administration canceled the B-1 bomber while failing in SALT negotiations to limit the Backfire (the first Soviet deep-penetration bomber capable of nuclear devastation of West European cities), except to insure that it should not be used against U.S. territory. Similarly, the United States hedges on development of the M-X missile and appears willing to re-

---

[88] Dewey, "The Nordic Balance," p. 51–52.

strict the range of the cruise missiles so vital to West European defense while declining to include in SALT II the Soviet "gray area systems" like the SS-20 mobile missile that are targeted on NATO Europe. Whatever the merits of the neutron bomb, the halfhearted U.S. campaign to win its acceptance in Europe and the abandonment of that campaign in the face of a concerted Soviet propaganda barrage bodes ill for future U.S. efforts to protect its NATO partners against Soviet force or intimidation. A position paper recently issued by the Coalition for Peace Through Strength notes that

> ... one of the most serious flaws of the SALT process has been its effect on ... NATO.... Militarily, the U.S. relationship with NATO has been based on the principle that U.S. strategic forces would serve as an umbrella or shield over Western Europe. NATO leaders are deeply ... distressed that the United States is considering a treaty that would lock NATO's only real nuclear power into a position of inferiority ...
>
> At present, NATO powers are concerned about what steps they should take ... to insure their survival in the absence of the U.S. strategic umbrella. One of their options is accommodation with the Communist bloc.[89]

Meanwhile, U.S. naval power has reportedly declined to the point where, under wartime conditions, a choice would probably have to be made between protecting the sea lines of communication (SLOCs) between North America and Europe or projecting naval power into Central Europe in support of NATO ground forces; in the past, the Navy was deemed capable of performing both missions. Furthermore, despite the phenomenal buildup of the USSR's Northern Fleet and the increasingly frequent Soviet forays beyond the Barents into the Greenland, Norwegian, and North seas and the Atlantic, the United States continues to deploy its strongest fleet in the

---

[89] *New York Times,* April 12, 1979.

Pacific, its second strongest in the Mediterranean, and the weakest of its three major fleets along the Atlantic lifeline of the NATO alliance. It is even questionable whether the understrength Second Fleet can reach the vital Greenland-Iceland-United Kingdom Gap (G-I-UK Gap) before the Soviet Navy does in the event of a crisis on NATO's northern flank. Coupled with rumors of U.S. reluctance to project naval (notably carrier-based) strength into the heavily defended Murmansk area, this power equation cannot but demoralize the northern flank states. This is particularly so in view of the use of the Soviet Navy as a political tool. "In the past decade, perhaps the most significant change in the Soviet Navy has been the alteration in its use from that of purely a wartime instrument to ... an instrument of major political influence as well. To that extent, Soviet naval power has become an ever more salient feature of the peacetime political environment in the North Atlantic and Nordic areas."[90]

There is a greater discrepancy between Soviet and Western forces along the northern flank than anywhere else in Europe, and this flank is the most heavily dependent of any region on early reinforcement. Since no local military balance exists, successful defense of the region is predicated upon Allied ability to secure control of the Norwegian and North seas and the airspace above them to insure the swift and steady flow of reinforcements to isolated Norway.

Soviet military capabilities along the northern flank have been described in detail, but Moscow's intentions remain a subject of great controversy in Scandinavia. It is this very uncertainty that contributes to the erosion of political stability in the Nordic countries, and this instability, in turn, furthers Soviet goals. As George Kennan has noted, "the technique of Russian diplomacy, like that of the Orient in general, is concentrated on impressing an adversary with the terrifying strength of Soviet power, while keeping him uncertain and confused as to the exact channels and means of its application and thus inducing him to treat all Russian wishes and views

---

[90] Myers, *North Atlantic Security*, p. 64.

with particular respect and consideration."[91] Russia's military buildup, coupled with Soviet propaganda, has been designed to impress upon the USSR's northern neighbors that resistance to Soviet power would be fruitless and that accommodation is the only logical course.

In view of their desire to achieve maximum politico-strategic gains at minimum risk and, especially, to avoid war with the United States, the Russians would like to obtain this accommodation peacefully. To do so, they attempt to manipulate the political, economic, and psychological currents in northern Europe to their advantage. In Leninist dogma, it is morally obligatory to exploit every weakness—be it military, political, or economic—in the enemy's posture. The countries along NATO's northern flank manifest an alarming combination of military unpreparedness, political vacillation, and economic fragility. In trying to meet the Soviet challenge, the northern flank states are hampered not only by military weakness but by a variety of domestic political factors: inflation, political resistance to increased defense spending, difficulty in recruiting enough lower-ranking noncommissioned officers, a yen for Scandinavian neutrality, deep-rooted pacifism, anti-German sentiment, a sense of cultural isolation from continental Europe, and a fear of provoking the USSR.

While Moscow carefully takes account of the overall situation in northern Europe and tailors its strategy and tactics accordingly, the United States tends to view Soviet moves along the northern flank in a purely military context, to pass off seemingly minor Soviet harassments as militarily insignificant, and to fail to appreciate the subtle shifting of the political outlook in the Nordic countries brought about by Soviet actions. The extent to which public attitudes have already been affected by growing Soviet military strength is reflected in the following front-page article that appeared in the conservative Norwegian daily *Morgenbladet* on October 8, 1975:

---

[91] Quoted in U.S. Senate, Committee on Government Operations, Subcommittee on National Security and International Operations, *International Negotiation: The Soviet Approach,* 1969, p. 4.

> The Soviets' intense buildup of naval power has given the East bloc a significant lead in the race for military supremacy on NATO's northern flank. The almost continuous Soviet maneuvers in the North Sea show that the Russians have built a mobile iron ring around Scandinavia. In reality, Norway, Denmark and Sweden now lie inside Soviet defense lines and outside those of the USA. Western military experts have increasingly begun to accept this opinion following a 50 percent expansion of the Soviet fleet in the last five years.

Even if unaccompanied by Soviet military pressure, Moscow's appeal to the Nordic countries to abandon their burdensome Western connections and live in peace with their friendly Soviet neighbor would evoke a powerful response in many Scandinavian circles. It is imperative for NATO to launch a political offensive of its own to match the Soviet campaign. The theme should be the continuing value—indeed, the absolute necessity—of the Western connection for the preservation of Scandinavian democracy. The political offensive should also encompass means to invalidate "the USSR's application of its own ground rules on NATO's flanks, i.e., that risks inherent in interference and influence-peddling diminish as one moves toward the edges of the Atlantic alliance."[92]

Perhaps the most vital ingredient in the proposed political offensive is an effort to overturn the perception that the northern flank lies behind a lengthening Soviet "Arctic Curtain" and that NATO, preoccupied with the central front, will prove unable and/or unwilling to come to the rescue if Moscow looses an avalanche. In fact, the glacier that could become an avalanche has already begun to move into Scandinavia, but its potential victims seem generally nonchalant. If the glacier encounters no obstacles in its path, it will continue to gather speed, leaving the Nordic peoples to gaze at it with a mixture of awe and helplessness. The Arctic Cur-

---

[92] Dewey, "The Nordic Balance," p. 58.

tain may soon block out the entire area from Svalbard to the southern tip of Denmark.

No military buttressing of the northern flank will suffice without an accompanying political and psychological reinforcement. Above all, NATO's northern partners (as well as the Soviet Union) must be convinced that Article 5 of the North Atlantic Treaty equating an attack upon one member as an attack upon all will be honored in time of need. The belief that the United States would not risk New York for Paris in a nuclear showdown was an important underlying current in France's decision to withdraw from the military structure of NATO. Today the question of whether America would "trade" its cities for Oslo or Copenhagen has assumed new urgency for the northern flank states.

There is an alarming indifference within the U.S. government in particular to the problem of defense of the northern flank. The Central Front has obvious priority, followed by the southern flank. Officials tend to display a combination of resignation to the indefensibility of Norway and Denmark with a belief that such incidents as snooping by Russian vessels off the Norwegian coast do not belie the view that overall Soviet intentions are benign. Yet, former NATO commander Haig believes that "we shall not have the luxury of a blatant cross-border operation in Central Europe, initiated and planned by the Soviet Union. Is it not more likely that we shall continue to be plagued by these ambiguous, ambivalent moves in which it is more difficult to assess our vital interest?"[93]

The lackadaisical American attitude is particularly incomprehensible in the light of history. The USSR (like tsarist Russia) has traditionally exerted pressure outward from its huge central core to influence political developments in neighboring states in a pro-Russian direction and, when possible, to annex territory along the periphery as buffer zones. The most recent examples of such annexation are the Baltic republics, eastern Poland, and parts of Finland, all of which relate directly to the geography of the northern flank. The USSR now appears

---
[93] *U.S. News & World Report,* March 1, 1976, p. 38.

poised to seek a protective cordon of "Finlandized" states along the periphery of the Warsaw Pact as an interim step toward asserting control over all of Western Europe. In case of war, northern Norway and other areas along the USSR's maritime frontiers would be priority targets. Yet, there is an inability and/or unwillingness in Washington to view Soviet "pinpricks" along the northern flank as salami tactics designed to soften up NATO's Norwegian arm and lop it off from the body of the alliance.

Even more ominous is a persistent inclination of U.S. policymakers to underestimate the significance of the northern flank and to view it as an auxiliary of the central front. It cannot be overemphasized that, far from constituting a dispensable area of Western defense whose neutralization would have an adverse psychological effect at most on NATO, the northern flank is the umbilical cord linking the United States and West Germany, the two strongest members of the alliance. Loss of this flank would prevent the reinforcement of German forces either through the Baltic or via Scandinavia and would render virtually impossible the U.S. ability to resupply its European allies by sea.

West Germany itself appears to harbor serious doubts about U.S. readiness to act quickly in case of a crisis in Europe. The general perception that the United States is committed to retrenchment abroad and is merely reacting (or, worse yet, failing to react) to Soviet military and diplomatic initiatives in various parts of the globe now appears applicable even to NATO territory. Thus, for example, when the U.S. and other NATO navies fail to show the flag in response to Soviet shows of strength off the Norwegian coast, not only the willingness but also the capability of Norway's Western allies to aid her in a crisis become open to question. Such U.S. passivity has helped to create a climate in which West German media caution against provoking the USSR with large-scale NATO maneuvers and in which officials of the ruling Social Democratic Party speak of loosening the Federal Republic's links with NATO and perhaps even opting for neutrality.

Whereas the USSR previously protested loudly at any hint

that Norway or Denmark would alter their "base and ban" policies, maintenance of these policies no longer appears sufficient; the countries' very links with NATO are now under Soviet attack. Moscow is also striving to effect the neutralization of the sparsely populated and poorly defended chain of Atlantic and Arctic islands that together form a bulwark against massive deployment of Soviet naval power into the Atlantic. Iceland, which has been termed an unsinkable aircraft carrier, is the most important of these islands. As a U.S. officer once said, without the U.S.-manned Keflavik airbase, "the Soviets would take Iceland and there would be no highway across the Atlantic. NATO would just wither away and die."[94] Iceland has also been dubbed the "cork in the bottle" that prevents the Soviet Navy from moving freely in and out of the Atlantic and along the sea lanes leading from that ocean in all directions.

The Keflavik base, however, has been a bone of contention in Icelandic politics since its establishment. The "cod wars" with Britain also soured Icelandic attitudes toward the Western alliance. Both the Icelandic economy and the political structure are precarious, and the Communists have a strong popular base. Soviet warships now exercise regularly in the waters east and southeast of Iceland, casting a shadow over the island's domestic landscape.

Iceland's withdrawal from NATO would be catastrophic for the West, even if the Russians did not immediately occupy the Keflavik base, for the island forms the central pillar of the so-called G-I-UK Gap, the major chokepoint through which Soviet naval forces would have to surge in order to reach the mid-Atlantic. Recent Soviet naval maneuvers indicate that the USSR is attempting to draw its forward defense line at the G-I-UK Gap, thus converting the Norwegian Sea into a Soviet lake and isolating Norway from the rest of NATO, as well as hindering NATO naval forces from approaching the vital military installations on the Kola Peninsula. Such a forward strategy, needless to say, carries political and psychological as well

---

[94] See the *New York Times,* November 22, 1971.

as military repercussions for the pro-Western islands in the area.

Across the Denmark Strait from Iceland lies Greenland, another component of the Gap that may be politically wobbly. The United States and Denmark share responsibility for Greenland's defense, and the firm attachment of the world's largest island to the NATO defense network has long been taken for granted. The airbase at Thule is almost exactly midway between Moscow and New York. Greenland also houses several radar and early warning installations and naval and air surveillance systems. Station Nord, a U.S.-built air strip in northeastern Greenland, is designed for the emergency use of bombers returning from missions over the Soviet Union. Small American forces are based at Thule and Sønderstrom.

New political and military factors on and around Greenland bode ill for Western security, however. Soviet submarines have increasingly moved westward from the Barents and Norwegian seas into the Greenland Sea for exercise and patrol and, perhaps, for eventual deployment as part of a "sanctuary." Moreover, there are reports that Soviet submarines have broken through under the polar icecap, through the Robeson Channel between Greenland and Ellesmere Island, to emerge at a location just off Disko, which hugs the southwestern coast of Greenland. Moscow has unsuccessfully sought Copenhagen's permission to establish meteorological stations on Greenland. Politically, a nascent Greenlandic nationalism has emerged, fed by Danish radicals and Soviet propaganda. Scattered protests have erupted on the island against NATO installations there. Most of the protests have been spearheaded by young Greenlanders who were exposed to Danish radical leftism while attending universities in Denmark. Exploitation of Greenland's oil, chrome, and other valuable resources could spark disputes of the kind now occurring between Norway and the Soviet Union in the Barents Sea and could lead the island's nationalists to demand independence as the only guarantee of full control over Greenland's mineral wealth. It is questionable whether the home rule just granted by Denmark will satisfy Greenland over the long run.

Scotland's relationship to the United Kingdom is not unlike that of Greenland to Denmark; thus, even the southern end of the G-I-UK Gap harbors political problems that jeopardize Western security interests. In addition, the strategic Shetland Islands are regarded as vulnerable to a Soviet blitzkrieg—an attack that would paralyze Britain's air defenses. Soviet warships regularly patrol the waters between Norway and Scotland. Soviet naval maneuvers off Scotland's northern coast in the spring of 1978 were viewed by West German and other NATO partners as a reflection of the U.S. Navy's declining ability to control the North Atlantic.

Other insular candidates for Soviet-inspired neutralization are Norwegian-controlled Jan Mayen Island, which has an airstrip and navigational stations, the Lofoten Islands off northwestern Norway, and Bear Island, which lies about halfway between Norway and Svalbard in the Barents Sea. The Soviet Union has already proposed a joint condominium with Norway for the defense of Bear Island. A potential conflict between Norway and Iceland over the dividing line between Iceland and Jan Mayen Island may also tempt Soviet meddlers.

Soviet efforts to undermine Norwegian sovereignty over Svalbard have already been described. This archipelago forms the northern end of another strategic chokepoint for Soviet naval forces leaving the Kola Peninsula. So far the Norwegians have been hampered from strengthening its defense because of their insistence of adhering strictly to the 1920 treaty that forbids military installations on the islands.

The Faeroe Islands, which belong to Denmark, may be yet another weak reed in the Western defense system. The USSR has played upon emergent Faeroese nationalism by hosting the islands' prime minister. A Communist party was created on the Faeroes in 1975. As Moscow is well aware, the islanders are resentful of Denmark's entry into NATO and inclusion of the Faeroes in the alliance's defense arrangements without consulting the local legislature. The Faeroese fear that such installations will make them major targets of Soviet attack in wartime. So far, Faeroese nationalism has been limited by the fact that large Danish subsidies are required to keep the economy on a sound footing. If significant quantities of oil or gas were discovered off the islands, however, the Faeroese might well demand home rule or even independence.

The brief preceding survey indicates that the USSR will spare no effort—consistent with its desire to avoid a direct military confrontation with the United States—in undermining the cohesion of NATO's northern flank. To the extent that NATO's attention remains riveted on the Central Front and that Soviet-American arrangements to stabilize central Europe occur at the expense of NATO's flanks, the opportunities for Soviet military probes and political subversion in the Nordic countries will increase. It is vital that the northern flank not be viewed as the line of least resistance as the USSR moves to expand the boundaries of its influence outward.

The term "flank" is itself misleading, for it implies an area of secondary or support operations. Perhaps NATO should adopt the Soviet concept of a TVD (theater of military operations), which, while functioning within the context of overall alliance strategy, is capable of carrying out its own specific military tasks on a self-sufficient basis, at least in the early stages of hostilities before reinforcements are needed. The USSR understands the importance of such an entity very well and, as noted above, is making great efforts to provide a defense in depth for its own northwestern TVD, while also using it as a base for offensive operations by land, sea, and air. Such a defense in depth is less feasible for Norway, with its back to the Kola Peninsula and the Soviet-dominated Barents Sea; but precisely for this reason NATO must formulate an effective strategy for priority reinforcement of the northern flank without neglecting other theaters.

This is not a study of possible scenarios in the northern theater, but it should be emphasized that here, as elsewhere, Soviet military doctrine postulates a short, very intense war aimed at creating territorial *faits accomplis* before the Nordic countries have the opportunity to mobilize or even to take the political steps necessary to bring their forces under NATO rather than national command. Such a strategy also puts on

NATO the onus of deciding on the first use of nuclear weapons.

Recent Soviet military writings have placed strong emphasis on the Manchurian campaign of 1945, implying that it may serve as a model for present-day campaigns in areas such as Norway. (The 1968 invasion of Czechoslovakia displayed many of the same features.) The salient characteristics of the Manchurian operation were the attainment of strategic surprise; the primacy of the offensive, employing massive—even redundant—forces; extensive use of deception and camouflage in the immediate pre-attack period; establishment of normal patterns of "defensive" deployments and exercises (mobilization by maneuver) well before the attack; assault by "combined arms"; and reliance on great mobility and intense firepower. The actual attack took the form of heavy bombardment, followed by a concentration of advance detachments of armored and mechanized columns along narrow breakthrough sectors, followed, in turn, by extremely rapid movement and deep penetration along multiple axes in order to seize key communication and control points and to envelop and destroy the enemy army. The main emphasis was on winning a decisive victory in the initial stages of the war and is particularly apropos to present-day conditions, when the USSR would strive for an unassailable first-phase lead before the economically and technologically superior West could bring its full weight to bear. Among the chief weaknesses of the Japanese Kwantung Army (and of NATO today) were the failure to prepare defenses in depth and to mobilize a larger share of its potential strength.

Today, the increasing westward movement of Soviet naval maneuvers, amphibious landing exercises, and air reconnaissance patterns creates difficulties in determining whether these movements are routine or signal the prelude to an attack. With warning time of the essence for NATO, especially along the vulnerable northern flank, the situation is exceedingly dangerous.

Soviet military writers have also given new emphasis to the Nazi blitzkrieg against Norway and Denmark in 1940 and its crucial role in facilitating German operations in Central and Western Europe. Moreover, the pattern of the Nazi landings was virtually duplicated during the *Sever* exercise of 1968 and *Okean* of 1970, when Soviet naval forces sailed out of the Baltic and along the Danish and Norwegian coasts to conduct amphibious landings on the Pechenga Peninsula, almost in view of Norwegian territory.

Also of direct relevance to the northern flank, in view of the USSR's naval buildup, are Soviet writings that stress the interdependence of sea supremacy and ground and air combat operations within a military theater. Once again invoking the lessons of history, a Soviet officer writes of the Russo-Japanese War of 1904–05: "Lenin saw in the seizure of sea supremacy by the Japanese Fleet favorable conditions for the successful accomplishment of other, more important operational and strategic missions: the occupation of Manchuria, the seizure of Sakhalin and Vladivostok, and the ultimate destruction of the Russian Army."[95] One can easily substitute the Soviet Northern Fleet for the Japanese Fleet, Norway and Denmark for Manchuria, Svalbard and other islands for Sakhalin (and the Kuriles), and the destruction of NATO for that of the tsarist army to relate this passage to the contemporary era.

Aside from the already-mentioned characteristics of Soviet military doctrine and strategy, it should be noted that nothing in Soviet military literature indicates that NATO will enjoy the luxury of fighting an isolated or limited battle on the northern flank. Soviet military strategists speak and write consistently of a "coalition war" between two blocs and of an attack along multiple axes. There is no mention of a limited war, either in terms of geography or of weapons employed. With special regard to the northern flank, the terrain of North Norway (frequently cited as the most likely spot for a limited Soviet military action) militates against blitzkrieg tactics, and the need to invade Finnish and Swedish territory to reach that

---

[95] Quoted in Captain First Rank Yu. Bystrov, "Winning Sea Supremacy," *Morskoi Sbornik,* No. 3, 1977, p. 26.

area would make the risks outweigh the benefits of a limited operation there.

John Erickson points out that the USSR's northwestern TVD possesses "substantial forces-in-being with rapid reinforcement facility, an advanced forward defense line and an increase in 'armament norms' [comprising that relative superiority] which would permit a full-scale effort against Scandinavia *in toto* via the northern areas and through the Baltic outlets, *even while mounting major operations in other sectors of the whole European theater.*"[96]

The Red Army's interlocking command structure greatly facilitates such a strategy, and the northern flank's need to compete with other sectors for available troops and supplies strongly enhances Moscow's chances for success. As one analyst observes, "NATO has demonstrated a surge capability in support of the northern flank should limited aggression occur. However, in the event of a concurrent Central European war, the northern flank is likely to be on its own."[97]

According to a usually reliable source, the Warsaw Pact has assigned 1.5 million troops (many of them Polish and East German) for a general attack on Scandinavia. The scenario reportedly calls for an assault against northern Sweden with heavy armored units from Finland, a naval thrust against Stockholm and Swedish and Danish islands in the Baltic, and Soviet paratroop landings behind Norwegian and Swedish lines, where the invaders would link up with local partisans who have been trained in special centers in the USSR and East Germany. Despite the hazards of Arctic warfare, as manifested in Russia's "Winter War" against Finland in 1939–40, Moscow and its Warsaw Pact allies expect to be able to occupy Scandinavia within 48 hours.[98]

Admiral Sergei Gorshkov's writings on the Soviet Navy imply still another source of danger for the northern flank. His articles (notably a series in 1972–73 in the journal *Morskoy*

---

[96] Erickson, "The Northern Theater," p. 6. Italics added.
[97] Christoph Bertram and Johan J. Holst, eds., *New Strategic Factors in the North Atlantic* (Oslo: Universitetsforlaget, 1977), p. 53.
[98] *Soviet Analyst,* February 8, 1979, p. 3.

Sbornik), coupled with Soviet naval deployments, suggest that, rather than stage an initial attack on the United States, the USSR will strike in Europe and withhold its SSBNs in a Barents Sea "sanctuary" to be used as a second strike force against the United States, a deterrent against U.S. involvement in Europe, or a bargaining chip in peace talks after Europe's submission. In view of the "sanctuary's" location in the very region where U.S. seaborne troops and supplies for the northern flank would have to land, the deterrent is indeed powerful.

Still other factors regarding Soviet strategy and doctrine should be mentioned in connection with the northern flank. One is that Soviet military writings stress the importance of directing the main attack at a place where the enemy least expects it. Commentators cite examples from World War II (the attack on the Germans at Stalingrad instead of to the west; the 1944 assault on Belorussia rather than to the south) to illustrate this point, but there is obvious relevance for today, when NATO's forces are most heavily concentrated along the inter-German border and the northern flank is little more than a tripwire. The Russians, in addition, have written extensively on the Maginot Line and its outflanking by Nazi forces pushing through the Benelux countries. It requires little imagination for Soviet forces similarly to outflank the Central Front by striking through Scandinavia. Finally, Lenin's doctrine of the weakest link, by which he referred to the position of the Western colonies in the chain of international monopoly capitalism, has military application as well. Just as it was postulated that depriving the "imperialists" of their overseas territories and markets would strangle the world capitalist system, so it can be seen that depriving the Atlantic Alliance of its northern flank would choke off the capacity of West Germany, NATO's heartland, to resist a Soviet onslaught. And as West Germany goes, so goes NATO.

A number of measures have already been implemented or planned to symbolize NATO's resolve and capacity to defend the northern flank. These include larger and more frequent maneuvers in both northern and southern Norway; greater

German participation in these maneuvers; more regular NATO naval exercises in the Norwegian Sea; an enhanced German naval presence in the Baltic and North seas; prestocking of heavy equipment in Scandinavia for Allied use; enhancement of reception facilities, such as ports and airfields, to permit the most rapid and efficacious unloading of NATO reinforcements to Norway and Denmark; some weapons standardization, such as purchase of the American F-16 aircraft by the Norwegian and Danish air forces; and utilization of the U.S. Marines in Norway, where they have undergone training for winter warfare. All these measures are essentially piecemeal, however. There still seems to be undue reliance in NATO quarters on sending to the northern flank whatever forces are available after meeting an expected Soviet invasion of Central Europe. Although a small number of U.S., Canadian, British, and Dutch forces are earmarked for immediate dispatch to Norway and Denmark, they can do little except help the undermanned Norwegian and Danish forces hold out until major reinforcements arrive, especially from the United States. In view of Soviet plans for a blitzkrieg, the possibility of Soviet interdiction of transatlantic sea- and airborne supplies, and Western reliance on considerable warning time and slow-moving mobilization procedures, such reinforcements may reach their destination to find Soviet troops on the doorstep.[99]

What is needed is a relatively self-sufficient northern flank within the context of overall NATO wartime operations and an enhanced U.S. ability to insure the free flow of equipment and communications from North America to West Germany via that flank. In view of the crucial importance of sea control along the northern flank and the basing there of the Soviet Union's most powerful fleet, British Vice-Admiral Sir James Jungius, Supreme Allied Commander Atlantic's Representative in Europe, has suggested creation of a permanent NATO

---

[99] It is generally estimated that Norwegian forces could hold out against a Soviet attack for two weeks without resupply or reinforcement; in the winter, they could probably hold out until the snow melted.

naval presence in the Norwegian Sea. This northern equivalent of the U.S. Sixth Fleet in the Mediterranean (along NATO's vulnerable southern flank) could, in Sir James's view, comprise British, German, Norwegian, Dutch, and perhaps Belgian ships, with additional vessels from the U.S. Navy when they could be spared from the Second Fleet in the Atlantic. Air cover for what Sir James dubs the maritime contingency force–Norwegian Sea (MARCONFORNOR) could be provided by Vertical/Short-Takeoff-and-Landing (VSTOL) aircraft on fleet components, by NATO maritime patrol planes based in the United Kingdom, Norway, and Iceland, and perhaps by other shore-based fighters.[100] Creation of a Norwegian Sea fleet would epitomize the fact that the most crucial aspect of warfare along the northern flank will be naval, with land and air operations aimed principally at furthering access to and control of the vital seas linking NATO's chief partners.

Whatever other instrumentalities might be employed for achieving NATO's objectives on the northern flank are best left to the alliance's military specialists—unhampered by the fears of U.S. and other Western politicians of provoking the USSR by a show of strength in NATO's own territory. For, as one specialist aptly points out, "the Soviet Union will continue her recent ruthless demonstrations of military power off the Danish and Norwegian coasts if ... such demonstrations result in good behavior in the Soviet sense rather than in a will to resist."[101]

Remote, inhospitable, and consisting predominantly of water, the vast region encompassing NATO's northern flank has long been underestimated in terms of military significance. When taken out of a vacuum and viewed in the context of a lifeline between the United States and NATO Europe, however, its importance is magnified manyfold. Even if Western complacency was justified when NATO navies held unchal-

---

[100] Vice-Admiral Sir James Jungius, "Maritime Aspects of the Northern Flank," *RUSI* (Journal of the Royal United Services Institute for Defence Studies), December 1978, p. 18–19.

[101] Vice-Admiral (Ret.) R. Steinhous, "The Northern Flank," unpublished paper, October 1977, p. 25–26.

lenged sway in the North Atlantic, it is no longer tolerable in the face of the growing Soviet threat:

> When viewed against the background of the change in the threat and projected on the Alliance as a whole... it becomes... clear why the Northern Flank has so long been regarded as a region of minor importance. For, as long as it could be assumed that the allied naval forces, in particular those of the U.S. and British navies, were sufficiently superior to the Russian Northern Fleet, the regional inferiority of NATO forces in Norway, Denmark and Schleswig-Holstein and the absence of local forces in Iceland were acceptable, because it was possible to offset these weaknesses quickly by the air offensive capabilities of carrier-borne air forces and to deploy reinforcements by sea at any time...
>
> Whereas in the past the problem was... that of a more or less regional threat to the territorial integrity of... Norway and Denmark, the present problem is... whether NATO is strong enough to keep intact the vital nerve of the Alliance to maintain control of the link between America and Europe.... If the North Atlantic were no longer to fulfill this function of a link, then a vital element of deterrence would be lost....[102]

Moreover, in conditions of actual warfare, "the Northern Flank is the left wing of the defensive front in Europe whose breakdown would shatter the capability of forward defense in the Central Region.... As long as the Northern Flank is controlled by NATO, it will be possible to preserve the continuity of overall operations in Northern and Central Europe and across the Atlantic Ocean, and there will be a possibility of direct mutual support."[103]

As Robert Weinland has pointed out, World War III may not be won on the northern flank, but it could definitely be

---

[102] *Ibid.*, p. 10–13.
[103] *Ibid.*, p. 22–23.

lost there.[104] If the USSR's expanding naval power, increasingly offensive-oriented airpower, and ground forces in the region convince the Nordic countries that U.S. power 4,000 miles distant is no match for Soviet strength in place, the war could be lost even before a shot is fired.

---

[104] See Robert Weinland, "War and Peace in the North: Some Political Implications of the Changing Military Situation in Northern Europe," Paper presented to the "Conference on the Nordic Balance in Perspective: The Changing Military and Political Situation," Center for Strategic and International Studies, Geoegetown University, Washington, D.C., June 15–16, 1978.

National Strategy Information Center, Inc.

PUBLICATIONS

Frank N. Trager, Editor
Dorothy E. Nicolosi, Associate Editor
Joyce E. Larson, Managing Editor

AGENDA PAPERS

The Soviet Threat to NATO's Northern Flank by Marian K. Leighton, November 1979
Does Defense Beggar Welfare? Myths Versus Realities by James L. Clayton, June 1979
Naval Race or Arms Control in the Indian Ocean? (Some Problems in Negotiating Naval Limitations) by Alvin J. Cottrell and Walter F. Hahn, September 1978
Power Projection: A Net Assessment of U.S. and Soviet Capabilities by W. Scott Thompson, April 1978
Understanding the Soviet Military Threat, How CIA Estimates Went Astray by William T. Lee, February 1977
Toward a New Defense for NATO, The Case for Tactical Nuclear Weapons, July 1976 (Out of print)
Seven Tracks to Peace in the Middle East by Frank R. Barnett, April 1975
Arms Treaties with Moscow: Unequal Terms Unevenly Applied? by Donald G. Brennan, April 1975 (Out of print)

Toward a U.S. Energy Policy by Klaus Knorr, March 1975 (Out of print)

Can We Avert Economic Warfare in Raw Materials? US Agriculture as a Blue Chip by William Schneider, July 1974

STRATEGY PAPERS

Raw Material Supply in a Multipolar World by Yuan-li Wu, October 1973. Revised edition, October 1979

India: Emergent Power? by Stephen P. Cohen and Richard L. Park, June 1978

The Kremlin and Labor: A Study in National Security Policy by Roy Godson, November 1977

The Evolution of Soviet Security Strategy 1965–1975 by Avigdor Haselkorn, November 1977

The Geopolitics of the Nuclear Era by Colin S. Gray, September 1977

The Sino-Soviet Confrontation: Implications for the Future by Harold C. Hinton, September 1976

Food, Foreign Policy, and Raw Materials Cartels by William Schneider, February 1976

Strategic Weapons: An Introduction by Norman Polmar, October 1975 (Out of print)

Soviet Sources of Military Doctrine and Strategy by William F. Scott, July 1975

Detente: Promises and Pitfalls by Gerald L. Steibel, March 1975 (Out of print)

Oil, Politics and Sea Power: The Indian Ocean Vortex by Ian W.A.C. Adie, December 1974 (Out of print)

The Soviet Presence in Latin America by James D. Theberge, June 1974

The Horn of Africa by J. Bowyer Bell, Jr., December 1973

Research and Development and the Prospects for International Security by Frederick Seitz and Rodney W. Nichols, December 1973

Other NSIC Publications

The People's Liberation Army: Communist China's Armed Forces by Angus M. Fraser, August 1973 (Out of print)

Nuclear Weapons and the Atlantic Alliance by Wynfred Joshua, May 1973

How to Think About Arms Control and Disarmament by James E. Dougherty, May 1973 (Out of print)

The Military Indoctrination of Soviet Youth by Leon Goure, January 1973 (Out of print)

The Asian Alliance: Japan and United States Policy by Franz Michael and Gaston J. Sigur, October 1972 (Out of print)

Iran, the Arabian Peninsula, and the Indian Ocean by R.M. Burrell and Alvin J. Cottrell, September 1972 (Out of print)

Soviet Naval Power: Challenge for the 1970s by Norman Polmar, April 1972. Revised edition, September 1974 (Out of print)

How Can We Negotiate with the Communists? by Gerald L. Steibel, March 1972 (Out of print)

Soviet Political Warfare Techniques, Espionage and Propaganda in the 1970s by Lyman B. Kirkpatrick, Jr., and Howland H. Sargeant, January 1972 (Out of print)

The Soviet Presence in the Eastern Mediterranean by Lawrence L. Whetten, September 1971 (Out of print)

The Military Unbalance: Is the U.S. Becoming a Second Class Power? June 1971 (Out of print)

The Future of South Vietnam by Brigadier F. P. Serong, February 1971 (Out of print)

Strategy and National Interests: Reflections for the Future by Bernard Brodie, January 1971 (Out of print)

The Mekong River: A Challenge in Peaceful Development for Southeast Asia by Eugene R. Black, December 1970 (Out of print)

Problems of Strategy in the Pacific and Indian Oceans by George G. Thomson, October 1970 (Out of print)

Soviet Penetration into the Middle East by Wynfred Joshua, July 1970. Revised edition, October 1971 (Out of print)

Australian Security Policies and Problems by Justus M. van der Kroef, May 1970 (Out of print)

Detente: Dilemma or Disaster? by Gerald L. Steibel, July 1969 (Out of print)

The Prudent Case for Safeguard by William R. Kintner, June 1969 (Out of print)

OTHER PUBLICATIONS

Intelligence Requirements for the 1980's: Elements of Intelligence edited by Roy Godson, October 1979

The Fateful Ends and Shades of SALT: Past... Present... And Yet to Come? by Paul H. Nitze, James E. Dougherty, and Francis X. Kane, March 1979

Strategic Options for the Early Eighties: What Can Be Done? edited by William R. Van Cleave and W. Scott Thompson, February 1979

Arms, Men, and Military Budgets: Issues for Fiscal Year 1979 by Francis P. Hoeber, David B. Kassing, and William Schneider, Jr., February 1978

Arms, Men, and Military Budgets: Issues for Fiscal Year 1978 edited by Francis P. Hoeber and William Schneider, Jr., May 1977

Oil, Divestiture and National Security edited by Frank N. Trager, December 1976

Arms, Men, and Military Budgets: Issues for Fiscal Year 1977 edited by William Schneider, Jr., and Francis P. Hoeber, May 1976

Indian Ocean Naval Limitations, Regional Issues and Global Implications by Alvin J. Cottrell and Walter F. Hahn, April 1976